# This planner belongs to :

______________________________

# Twenty-one

## January

| S | M | T | W | T | F | S |
|---|---|---|---|---|---|---|
|  |  |  |  |  | 1 | 2 |
| 3 | 4 | 5 | 6 | 7 | 8 | 9 |
| 10 | 11 | 12 | 13 | 14 | 15 | 16 |
| 17 | 18 | 19 | 20 | 21 | 22 | 23 |
| 24 | 25 | 26 | 27 | 28 | 29 | 30 |
| 31 |  |  |  |  |  |  |

## February

| S | M | T | W | T | F | S |
|---|---|---|---|---|---|---|
|  | 1 | 2 | 3 | 4 | 5 | 6 |
| 7 | 8 | 9 | 10 | 11 | 12 | 13 |
| 14 | 15 | 16 | 17 | 18 | 19 | 20 |
| 21 | 22 | 23 | 24 | 25 | 26 | 27 |
| 28 |  |  |  |  |  |  |

## March

| S | M | T | W | T | F | S |
|---|---|---|---|---|---|---|
|  | 1 | 2 | 3 | 4 | 5 | 6 |
| 7 | 8 | 9 | 10 | 11 | 12 | 13 |
| 14 | 15 | 16 | 17 | 18 | 19 | 20 |
| 21 | 22 | 23 | 24 | 25 | 26 | 27 |
| 28 | 29 | 30 | 31 |  |  |  |

## April

| S | M | T | W | T | F | S |
|---|---|---|---|---|---|---|
|  |  |  |  | 1 | 2 | 3 |
| 4 | 5 | 6 | 7 | 8 | 9 | 10 |
| 11 | 12 | 13 | 14 | 15 | 16 | 17 |
| 18 | 19 | 20 | 21 | 22 | 23 | 24 |
| 25 | 26 | 27 | 28 | 29 | 30 |  |

## May

| S | M | T | W | T | F | S |
|---|---|---|---|---|---|---|
|  |  |  |  |  |  | 1 |
| 2 | 3 | 4 | 5 | 6 | 7 | 8 |
| 9 | 10 | 11 | 12 | 13 | 14 | 15 |
| 16 | 17 | 18 | 19 | 20 | 21 | 22 |
| 23 | 24 | 25 | 26 | 27 | 28 | 29 |
| 30 | 31 |  |  |  |  |  |

## June

| S | M | T | W | T | F | S |
|---|---|---|---|---|---|---|
|  |  | 1 | 2 | 3 | 4 | 5 |
| 6 | 7 | 8 | 9 | 10 | 11 | 12 |
| 13 | 14 | 15 | 16 | 17 | 18 | 19 |
| 20 | 21 | 22 | 23 | 24 | 25 | 26 |
| 27 | 28 | 29 | 30 |  |  |  |

## July

| S | M | T | W | T | F | S |
|---|---|---|---|---|---|---|
|  |  |  |  | 1 | 2 | 3 |
| 4 | 5 | 6 | 7 | 8 | 9 | 10 |
| 11 | 12 | 13 | 14 | 15 | 16 | 17 |
| 18 | 19 | 20 | 21 | 22 | 23 | 24 |
| 25 | 26 | 27 | 28 | 29 | 30 | 31 |

## August

| S | M | T | W | T | F | S |
|---|---|---|---|---|---|---|
| 1 | 2 | 3 | 4 | 5 | 6 | 7 |
| 8 | 9 | 10 | 11 | 12 | 13 | 14 |
| 15 | 16 | 17 | 18 | 19 | 20 | 21 |
| 22 | 23 | 24 | 25 | 26 | 27 | 28 |
| 29 | 30 | 31 |  |  |  |  |

## September

| S | M | T | W | T | F | S |
|---|---|---|---|---|---|---|
|  |  |  | 1 | 2 | 3 | 4 |
| 5 | 6 | 7 | 8 | 9 | 10 | 11 |
| 12 | 13 | 14 | 15 | 16 | 17 | 18 |
| 19 | 20 | 21 | 22 | 23 | 24 | 25 |
| 26 | 27 | 28 | 29 | 30 |  |  |

## October

| S | M | T | W | T | F | S |
|---|---|---|---|---|---|---|
|  |  |  |  |  | 1 | 2 |
| 3 | 4 | 5 | 6 | 7 | 8 | 9 |
| 10 | 11 | 12 | 13 | 14 | 15 | 16 |
| 17 | 18 | 19 | 20 | 21 | 22 | 23 |
| 24 | 25 | 26 | 27 | 28 | 29 | 30 |
| 31 |  |  |  |  |  |  |

## November

| S | M | T | W | T | F | S |
|---|---|---|---|---|---|---|
|  | 1 | 2 | 3 | 4 | 5 | 6 |
| 7 | 8 | 9 | 10 | 11 | 12 | 13 |
| 14 | 15 | 16 | 17 | 18 | 19 | 20 |
| 21 | 22 | 23 | 24 | 25 | 26 | 27 |
| 28 | 29 | 30 |  |  |  |  |

## December

| S | M | T | W | T | F | S |
|---|---|---|---|---|---|---|
|  |  |  | 1 | 2 | 3 | 4 |
| 5 | 6 | 7 | 8 | 9 | 10 | 11 |
| 12 | 13 | 14 | 15 | 16 | 17 | 18 |
| 19 | 20 | 21 | 22 | 23 | 24 | 25 |
| 26 | 27 | 28 | 29 | 30 | 31 |  |

# Year in Pixels

|  | J | F | M | A | M | J | J | A | S | O | N | D |
|---|---|---|---|---|---|---|---|---|---|---|---|---|
| 1. | | | | | | | | | | | | |
| 2. | | | | | | | | | | | | |
| 3. | | | | | | | | | | | | |
| 4. | | | | | | | | | | | | |
| 5. | | | | | | | | | | | | |
| 6. | | | | | | | | | | | | |
| 7. | | | | | | | | | | | | |
| 8. | | | | | | | | | | | | |
| 9. | | | | | | | | | | | | |
| 10. | | | | | | | | | | | | |
| 11. | | | | | | | | | | | | |
| 12. | | | | | | | | | | | | |
| 13. | | | | | | | | | | | | |
| 14. | | | | | | | | | | | | |
| 15. | | | | | | | | | | | | |
| 16. | | | | | | | | | | | | |
| 17. | | | | | | | | | | | | |
| 18. | | | | | | | | | | | | |
| 19. | | | | | | | | | | | | |
| 20. | | | | | | | | | | | | |
| 21. | | | | | | | | | | | | |
| 22. | | | | | | | | | | | | |
| 23. | | | | | | | | | | | | |
| 24. | | | | | | | | | | | | |
| 25. | | | | | | | | | | | | |
| 26. | | | | | | | | | | | | |
| 27. | | | | | | | | | | | | |
| 28. | | | | | | | | | | | | |
| 29. | | | | | | | | | | | | |
| 30. | | | | | | | | | | | | |
| 31. | | | | | | | | | | | | |

## Color Codes

## Notes

# January 2021

| SUNDAY | MONDAY | TUESDAY | WEDNESDAY |
|---|---|---|---|
|  |  |  |  |
| 3 | 4 | 5 | 6 |
| 10 | 11 | 12 | 13 |
| 17 | 18 | 19 | 20 |
| 24 | 25 | 26 | 27 |

# January 2021

| THURSDAY | FRIDAY | SATURDAY | NOTES |
|---|---|---|---|
|  | 1 | 2 | ○ |
|  |  |  | ○ |
|  |  |  | ○ |
|  |  |  | ○ |
| 7 | 8 | 9 | ○ |
|  |  |  | ○ |
|  |  |  | ○ |
|  |  |  | ○ |
| 14 | 15 | 16 | ○ |
|  |  |  | ○ |
|  |  |  | ○ |
|  |  |  | ○ |
| 21 | 22 | 23 | ○ |
|  |  |  | ○ |
|  |  |  | ○ |
|  |  |  | ○ |
|  |  |  | ○ |
| 28 | 29 | 30 | 31 |

# February 2021

| SUNDAY | MONDAY | TUESDAY | WEDNESDAY |
|---|---|---|---|
|  | 1 | 2 | 3 |
| 7 | 8 | 9 | 10 |
| 14 | 15 | 16 | 17 |
| 21 | 22 | 23 | 24 |
| 28 |  |  |  |

# February 2021

| THURSDAY | FRIDAY | SATURDAY | NOTES |
|---|---|---|---|
| 4 | 5 | 6 | ○ |
|  |  |  | ○ |
|  |  |  | ○ |
|  |  |  | ○ |
|  |  |  | ○ |
|  |  |  | ○ |
| 11 | 12 | 13 | ○ |
|  |  |  | ○ |
|  |  |  | ○ |
|  |  |  | ○ |
| 18 | 19 | 20 | ○ |
|  |  |  | ○ |
|  |  |  | ○ |
|  |  |  | ○ |
|  |  |  | ○ |
| 25 | 26 | 27 | ○ |
|  |  |  | ○ |
|  |  |  | ○ |
|  |  |  | ○ |
|  |  |  | ○ |
|  |  |  | NOTES |

# March 2021

| SUNDAY | MONDAY | TUESDAY | WEDNESDAY |
|---|---|---|---|
|  | 1 | 2 | 3 |
| 7 | 8 | 9 | 10 |
| 14 | 15 | 16 | 17 |
| 21 | 22 | 23 | 24 |
| 28 | 29 | 30 | 31 |

# March 2021

| THURSDAY | FRIDAY | SATURDAY | NOTES |
|---|---|---|---|
| 4 | 5 | 6 | ○ |
|  |  |  | ○ |
|  |  |  | ○ |
|  |  |  | ○ |
|  |  |  | ○ |
| 11 | 12 | 13 | ○ |
|  |  |  | ○ |
|  |  |  | ○ |
|  |  |  | ○ |
| 18 | 19 | 20 | ○ |
|  |  |  | ○ |
|  |  |  | ○ |
|  |  |  | ○ |
| 25 | 26 | 27 | ○ |
|  |  |  | ○ |
|  |  |  | ○ |
|  |  |  | ○ |
|  |  |  | ○ |
|  |  |  | NOTES |

# April 2021

| SUNDAY | MONDAY | TUESDAY | WEDNESDAY |
|---|---|---|---|
|  |  |  |  |
| 4 | 5 | 6 | 7 |
| 11 | 12 | 13 | 14 |
| 18 | 19 | 20 | 21 |
| 25 | 26 | 27 | 28 |

# April 2021

| THURSDAY | FRIDAY | SATURDAY | NOTES |
|---|---|---|---|
| 1 | 2 | 3 | ○ |
|  |  |  | ○ |
|  |  |  | ○ |
|  |  |  | ○ |
|  |  |  | ○ |
| 8 | 9 | 10 | ○ |
|  |  |  | ○ |
|  |  |  | ○ |
|  |  |  | ○ |
| 15 | 16 | 17 | ○ |
|  |  |  | ○ |
|  |  |  | ○ |
|  |  |  | ○ |
|  |  |  | ○ |
| 22 | 23 | 24 | ○ |
|  |  |  | ○ |
|  |  |  | ○ |
|  |  |  | ○ |
|  |  |  | ○ |
| 29 | 30 | 1 | NOTES |

# May



| SUNDAY | MONDAY | TUESDAY | WEDNESDAY |
|---|---|---|---|
| 2 | 3 | 4 | 5 |
| 9 | 10 | 11 | 12 |
| 16 | 17 | 18 | 19 |
| 23 | 24 | 25 | 26 |
| 30 | 31 | | |

# May 2021

| THURSDAY | FRIDAY | SATURDAY | NOTES |
|---|---|---|---|
| 6 | 7 | 8 | ○ |
| 13 | 14 | 15 | ○ ○ ○ ○ ○ |
| 20 | 21 | 22 | ○ ○ ○ ○ ○ |
| 27 | 28 | 29 | ○ ○ ○ ○ ○ |
| | | | NOTES |

# June 2021

| SUNDAY | MONDAY | TUESDAY | WEDNESDAY |
| --- | --- | --- | --- |
|  |  | 1 | 2 |
| 6 | 7 | 8 | 9 |
| 13 | 14 | 15 | 16 |
| 20 | 21 | 22 | 23 |
| 27 | 28 | 29 | 30 |

# June 2021

| THURSDAY | FRIDAY | SATURDAY | NOTES |
|---|---|---|---|
| 3 | 4 | 5 | ○ |
| | | | ○ |
| | | | ○ |
| | | | ○ |
| | | | ○ |
| 10 | 11 | 12 | ○ |
| | | | ○ |
| | | | ○ |
| | | | ○ |
| 17 | 18 | 19 | ○ |
| | | | ○ |
| | | | ○ |
| | | | ○ |
| | | | ○ |
| 24 | 25 | 26 | ○ |
| | | | ○ |
| | | | ○ |
| | | | ○ |
| | | | ○ |
| | | | NOTES |

# July 2021

| SUNDAY | MONDAY | TUESDAY | WEDNESDAY |
|---|---|---|---|
|  |  |  |  |
| 4 | 5 | 6 | 7 |
| 11 | 12 | 13 | 14 |
| 18 | 19 | 20 | 21 |
| 25 | 26 | 27 | 28 |

# July 2021

| THURSDAY | FRIDAY | SATURDAY | NOTES |
| --- | --- | --- | --- |
| 1 | 2 | 3 | ○ |
| | | | ○ |
| | | | ○ |
| | | | ○ |
| | | | ○ |
| 8 | 9 | 10 | ○ |
| | | | ○ |
| | | | ○ |
| | | | ○ |
| | | | ○ |
| 15 | 16 | 17 | ○ |
| | | | ○ |
| | | | ○ |
| | | | ○ |
| | | | ○ |
| 22 | 23 | 24 | ○ |
| | | | ○ |
| | | | ○ |
| | | | ○ |
| | | | ○ |
| 29 | 30 | 31 | NOTES |

# August 2021

| SUNDAY | MONDAY | TUESDAY | WEDNESDAY |
| --- | --- | --- | --- |
| 1 | 2 | 3 | 4 |
| 8 | 9 | 10 | 11 |
| 15 | 16 | 17 | 18 |
| 22 | 23 | 24 | 25 |
| 29 | 30 | 31 | |

# August 2021

| THURSDAY | FRIDAY | SATURDAY | NOTES |
|---|---|---|---|
| 5 | 6 | 7 | ○ |
|  |  |  | ○ |
|  |  |  | ○ |
|  |  |  | ○ |
|  |  |  | ○ |
| 12 | 13 | 14 | ○ |
|  |  |  | ○ |
|  |  |  | ○ |
|  |  |  | ○ |
| 19 | 20 | 21 | ○ |
|  |  |  | ○ |
|  |  |  | ○ |
|  |  |  | ○ |
|  |  |  | ○ |
| 26 | 27 | 28 | NOTES |
|  |  |  |  |

# September 2021

| SUNDAY | MONDAY | TUESDAY | WEDNESDAY |
|---|---|---|---|
|  |  |  | 1 |
| 5 | 6 | 7 | 8 |
| 12 | 13 | 14 | 15 |
| 19 | 20 | 21 | 22 |
| 26 | 27 | 28 | 29 |

# September 2021

| THURSDAY | FRIDAY | SATURDAY | NOTES |
|---|---|---|---|
| 2 | 3 | 4 | ○ |
|  |  |  | ○ |
|  |  |  | ○ |
|  |  |  | ○ |
|  |  |  | ○ |
| 9 | 10 | 11 | ○ |
|  |  |  | ○ |
|  |  |  | ○ |
|  |  |  | ○ |
| 16 | 17 | 18 | ○ |
|  |  |  | ○ |
|  |  |  | ○ |
|  |  |  | ○ |
|  |  |  | ○ |
| 23 | 24 | 25 | ○ |
|  |  |  | ○ |
|  |  |  | ○ |
|  |  |  | ○ |
|  |  |  | ○ |
| 30 |  |  | NOTES |

# October 2021

| SUNDAY | MONDAY | TUESDAY | WEDNESDAY |
| --- | --- | --- | --- |
|  |  |  |  |
| 3 | 4 | 5 | 6 |
| 10 | 11 | 12 | 13 |
| 17 | 18 | 19 | 20 |
| 24 | 25 | 26 | 27 |

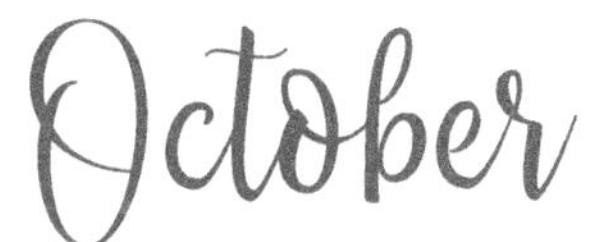

# October 2021

| THURSDAY | FRIDAY | SATURDAY | NOTES |
|---|---|---|---|
| | 1 | 2 | ○ |
| | | | ○ |
| | | | ○ |
| | | | ○ |
| | | | ○ |
| 7 | 8 | 9 | ○ |
| | | | ○ |
| | | | ○ |
| | | | ○ |
| 14 | 15 | 16 | ○ |
| | | | ○ |
| | | | ○ |
| | | | ○ |
| | | | ○ |
| 21 | 22 | 23 | ○ |
| | | | ○ |
| | | | ○ |
| | | | ○ |
| | | | ○ |
| 28 | 29 | 30 / 31 SUNDAY | NOTES |

# November 2021

| SUNDAY | MONDAY | TUESDAY | WEDNESDAY |
|---|---|---|---|
|  | 1 | 2 | 3 |
| 7 | 8 | 9 | 10 |
| 14 | 15 | 16 | 17 |
| 21 | 22 | 23 | 24 |
| 28 | 29 | 30 |  |

# November 2021

| THURSDAY | FRIDAY | SATURDAY | NOTES |
|---|---|---|---|
| 4 | 5 | 6 | ○ |
| | | | ○ |
| | | | ○ |
| | | | ○ |
| | | | ○ |
| 11 | 12 | 13 | ○ |
| | | | ○ |
| | | | ○ |
| | | | ○ |
| 18 | 19 | 20 | ○ |
| | | | ○ |
| | | | ○ |
| | | | ○ |
| | | | ○ |
| 25 | 26 | 27 | ○ |
| | | | ○ |
| | | | ○ |
| | | | ○ |
| | | | ○ |
| | | | NOTES |

# December 2021

| SUNDAY | MONDAY | TUESDAY | WEDNESDAY |
|---|---|---|---|
|  |  |  | 1 |
| 5 | 6 | 7 | 8 |
| 12 | 13 | 14 | 15 |
| 19 | 20 | 21 | 22 |
| 26 | 27 | 28 | 29 |

# December 2021

| THURSDAY | FRIDAY | SATURDAY | NOTES |
|---|---|---|---|
| 2 | 3 | 4 | ○ |
| | | | ○ |
| | | | ○ |
| | | | ○ |
| | | | ○ |
| 9 | 10 | 11 | ○ |
| | | | ○ |
| | | | ○ |
| | | | ○ |
| | | | ○ |
| 16 | 17 | 18 | ○ |
| | | | ○ |
| | | | ○ |
| | | | ○ |
| | | | ○ |
| 23 | 24 | 25 | ○ |
| | | | ○ |
| | | | ○ |
| | | | ○ |
| | | | ○ |
| 30 | 31 | | NOTES |

**01** TUESDAY

**02** WEDNESDAY

**03** THURSDAY

**04** FRIDAY

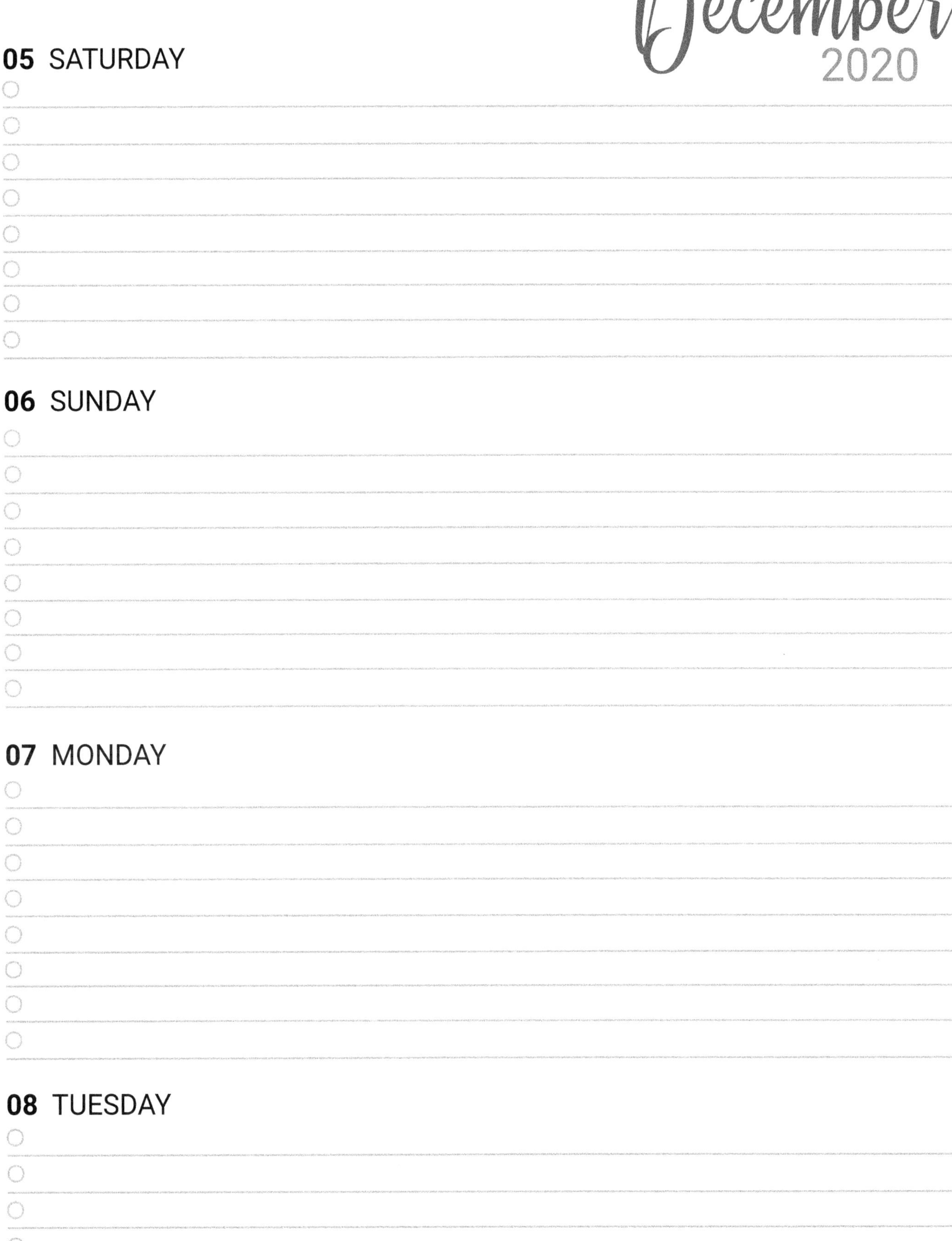


December
2020

**05** SATURDAY

**06** SUNDAY

**07** MONDAY

**08** TUESDAY

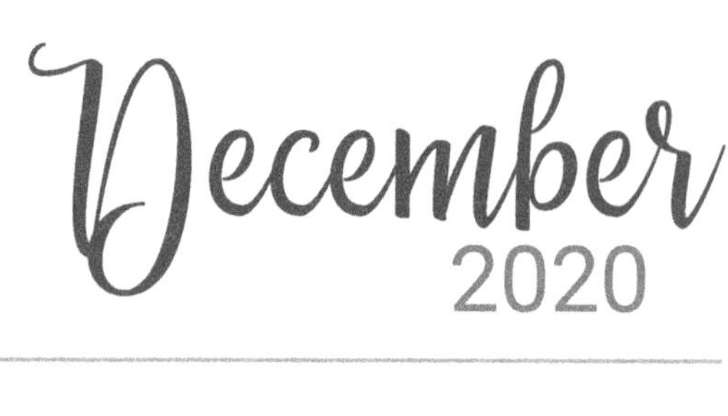


**09** WEDNESDAY

**10** THURSDAY

**11** FRIDAY

**12** SATURDAY

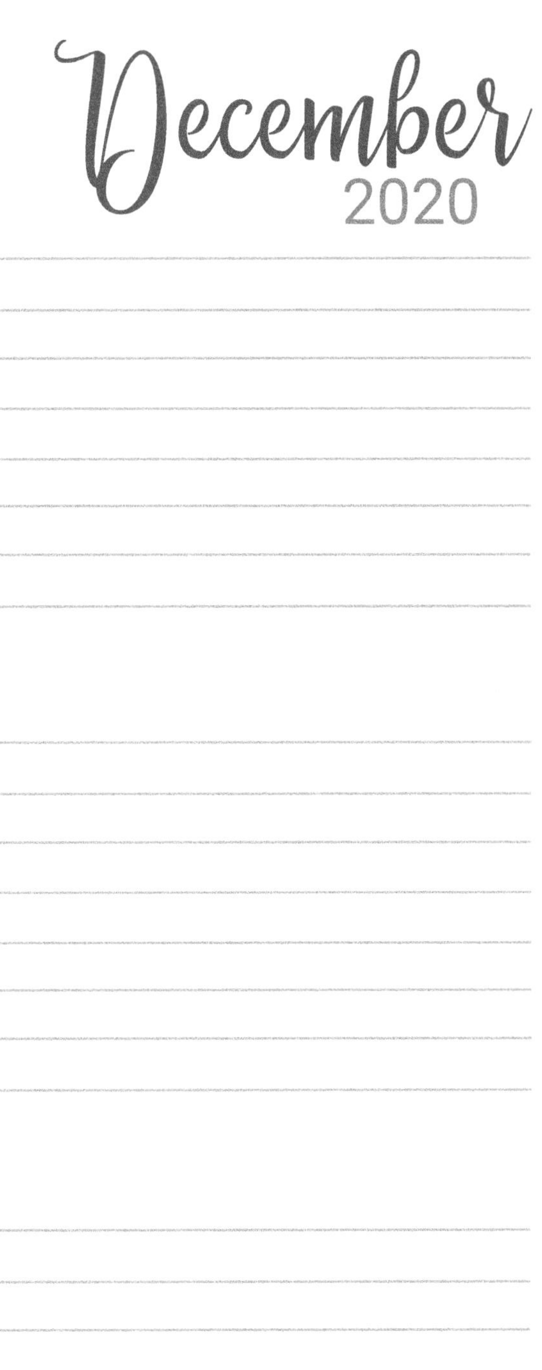

## 13 SUNDAY

## 14 MONDAY

## 15 TUESDAY

## 16 WEDNESDAY

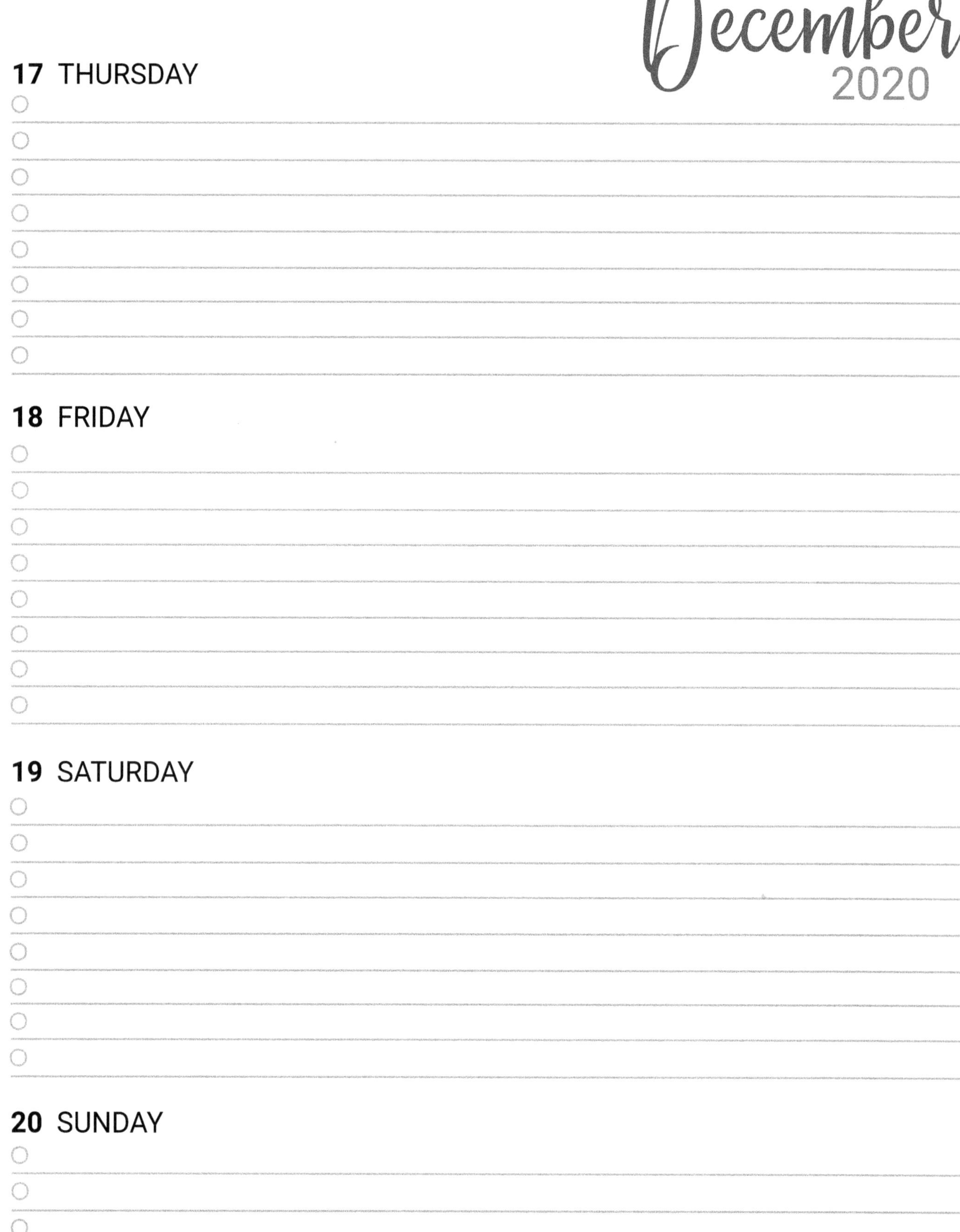



**17** THURSDAY

**18** FRIDAY

**19** SATURDAY

**20** SUNDAY

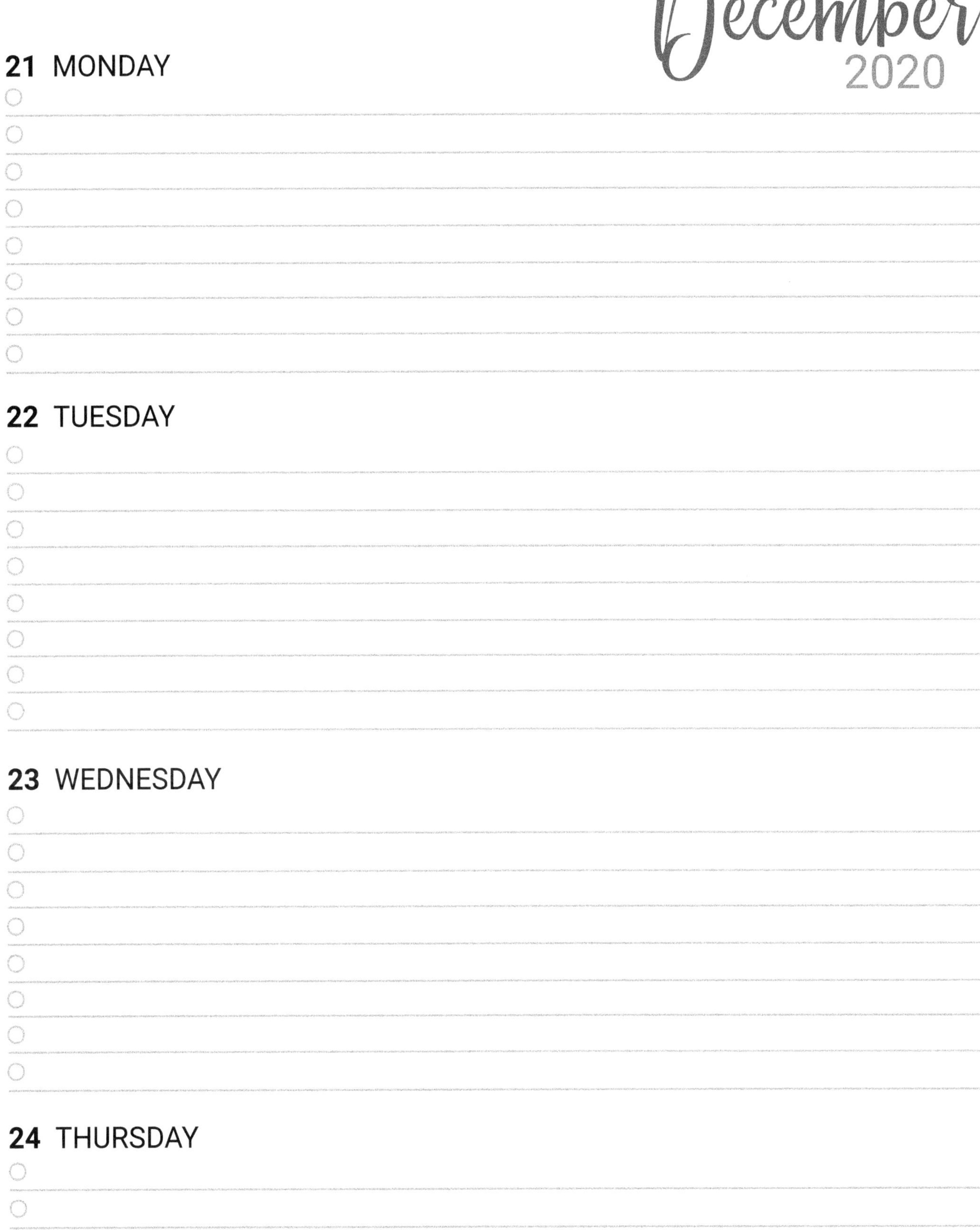



**21** MONDAY

**22** TUESDAY

**23** WEDNESDAY

**24** THURSDAY

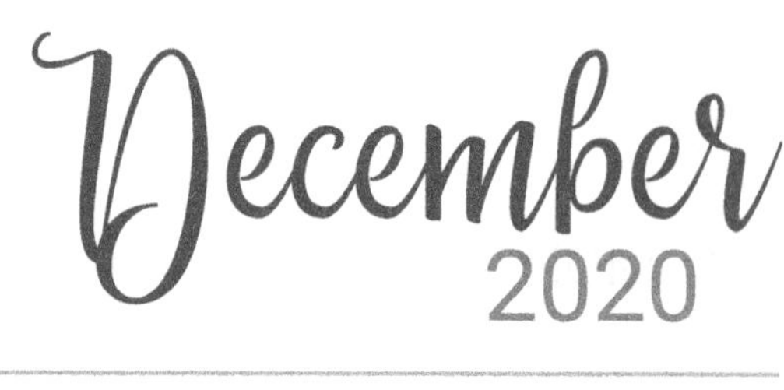


**25** FRIDAY

**26** SATURDAY

**27** SUNDAY

**28** MONDAY

**29** TUESDAY

**30** WEDNESDAY

**31** THURSDAY

NOTES

**01** FRIDAY

**02** SATURDAY

**03** SUNDAY

**04** MONDAY

# January
## 2021

**05** TUESDAY

**06** WEDNESDAY

**07** THURSDAY

**08** FRIDAY

**09** SATURDAY

**10** SUNDAY

**11** MONDAY

**12** TUESDAY

**13** WEDNESDAY

**14** THURSDAY

**15** FRIDAY

**16** SATURDAY

**17** SUNDAY

**18** MONDAY

**19** TUESDAY

**20** WEDNESDAY

**21** THURSDAY

**22** FRIDAY

**23** SATURDAY

**24** SUNDAY

**25** MONDAY

**26** TUESDAY

**27** WEDNESDAY

**28** THURSDAY

**29** FRIDAY

**30** SATURDAY

**31** SUNDAY

NOTES

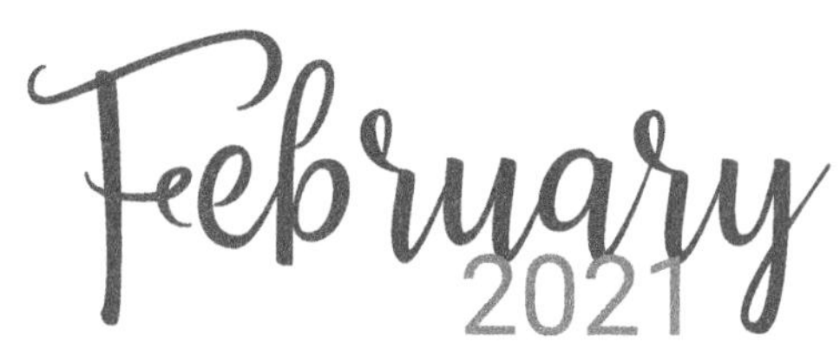

**01** MONDAY

**02** TUESDAY

**03** WEDNESDAY

**04** THURSDAY

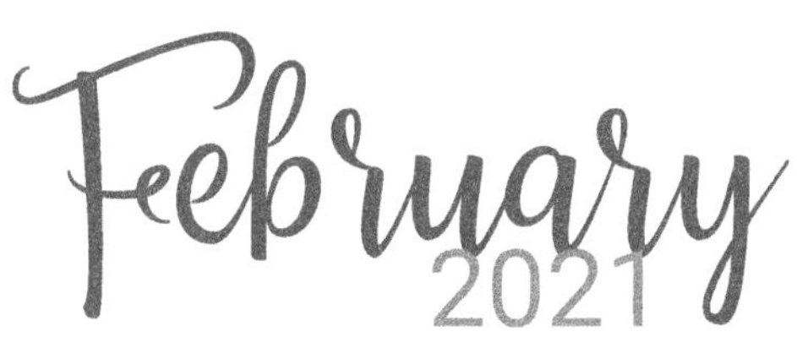

**05** FRIDAY

**06** SATURDAY

**07** SUNDAY

**08** MONDAY

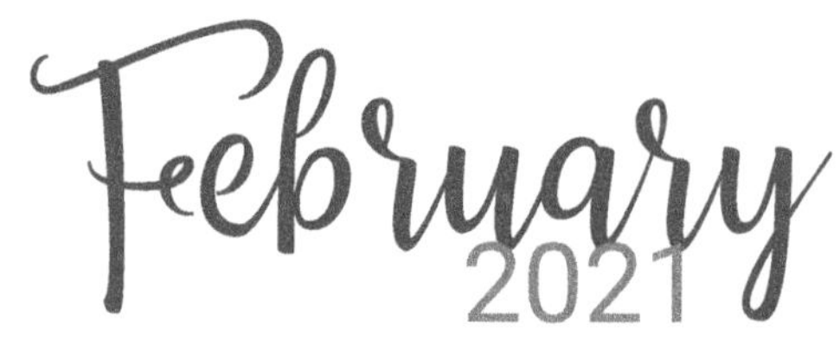


**09** TUESDAY

**10** WEDNESDAY

**11** THURSDAY

**12** FRIDAY

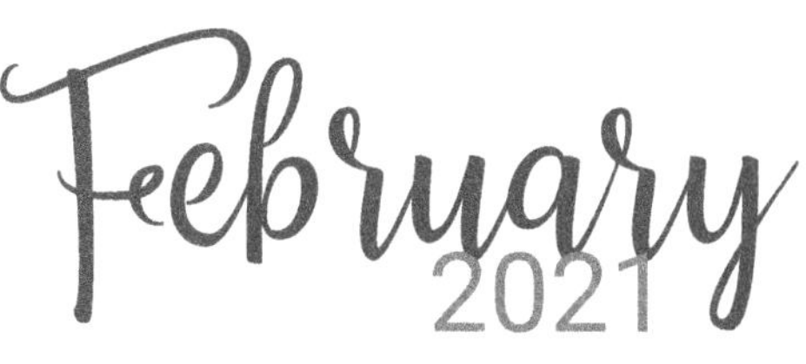



## 13 SATURDAY

## 14 SUNDAY

## 15 MONDAY

## 16 TUESDAY

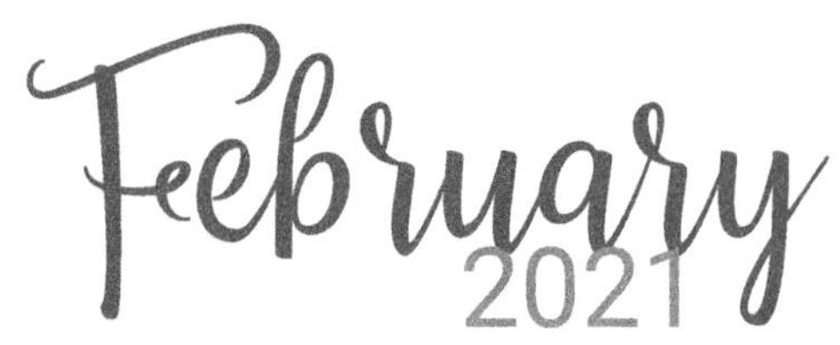


**17** WEDNESDAY

**18** THURSDAY

**19** FRIDAY

**20** SATURDAY

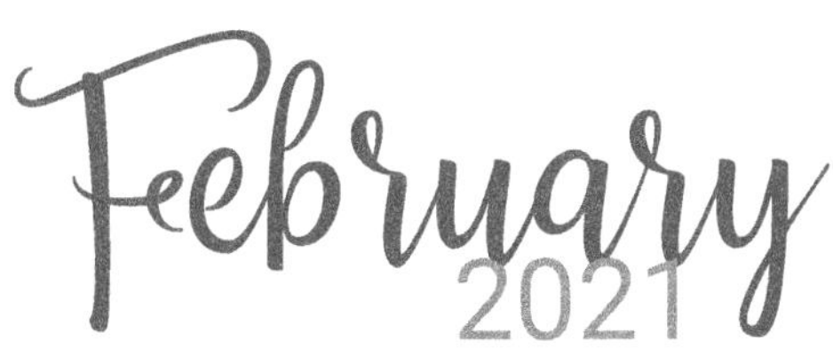

# February
## 2021

**21** SUNDAY

**22** MONDAY

**23** TUESDAY

**24** WEDNESDAY

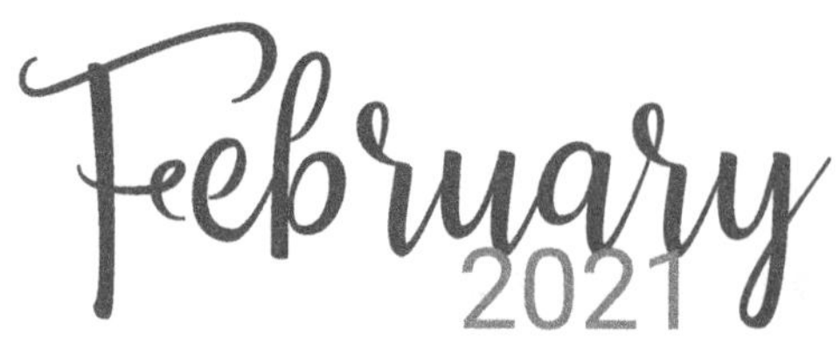


## 25 THURSDAY

## 26 FRIDAY

## 27 SATURDAY

## 28 SUNDAY

**01** MONDAY

**02** TUESDAY

**03** WEDNESDAY

**04** THURSDAY

**05** FRIDAY

**06** SATURDAY

**07** SUNDAY

**08** MONDAY

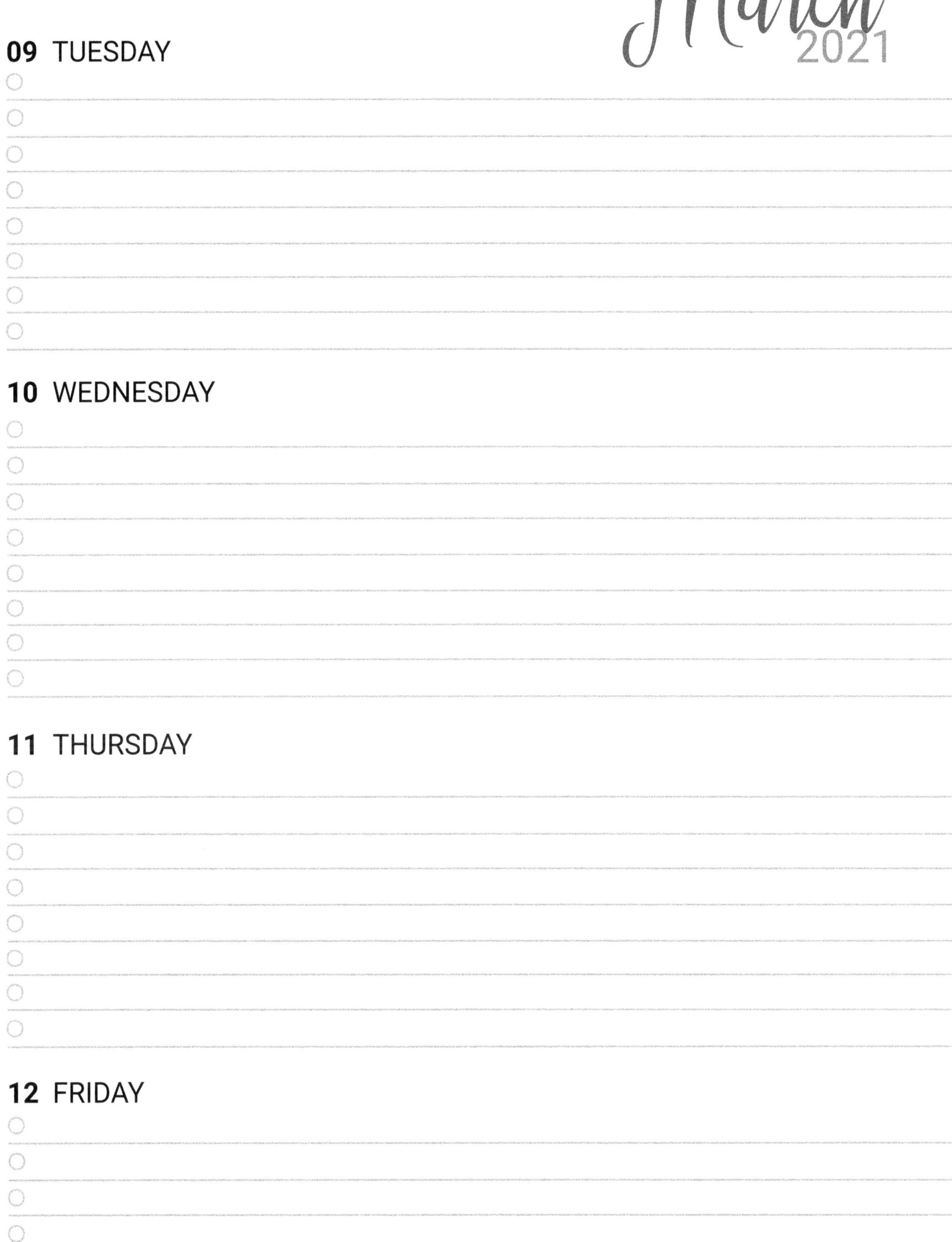

# March
## 2021

**09** TUESDAY

**10** WEDNESDAY

**11** THURSDAY

**12** FRIDAY

**13** SATURDAY

**14** SUNDAY

**15** MONDAY

**16** TUESDAY

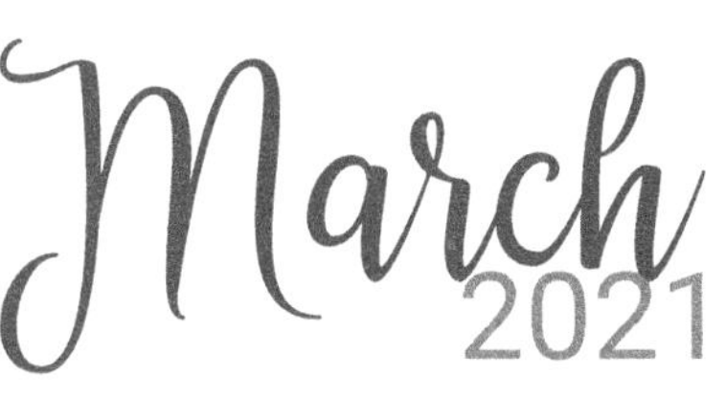



## 17 WEDNESDAY

## 18 THURSDAY

## 19 FRIDAY

## 20 SATURDAY

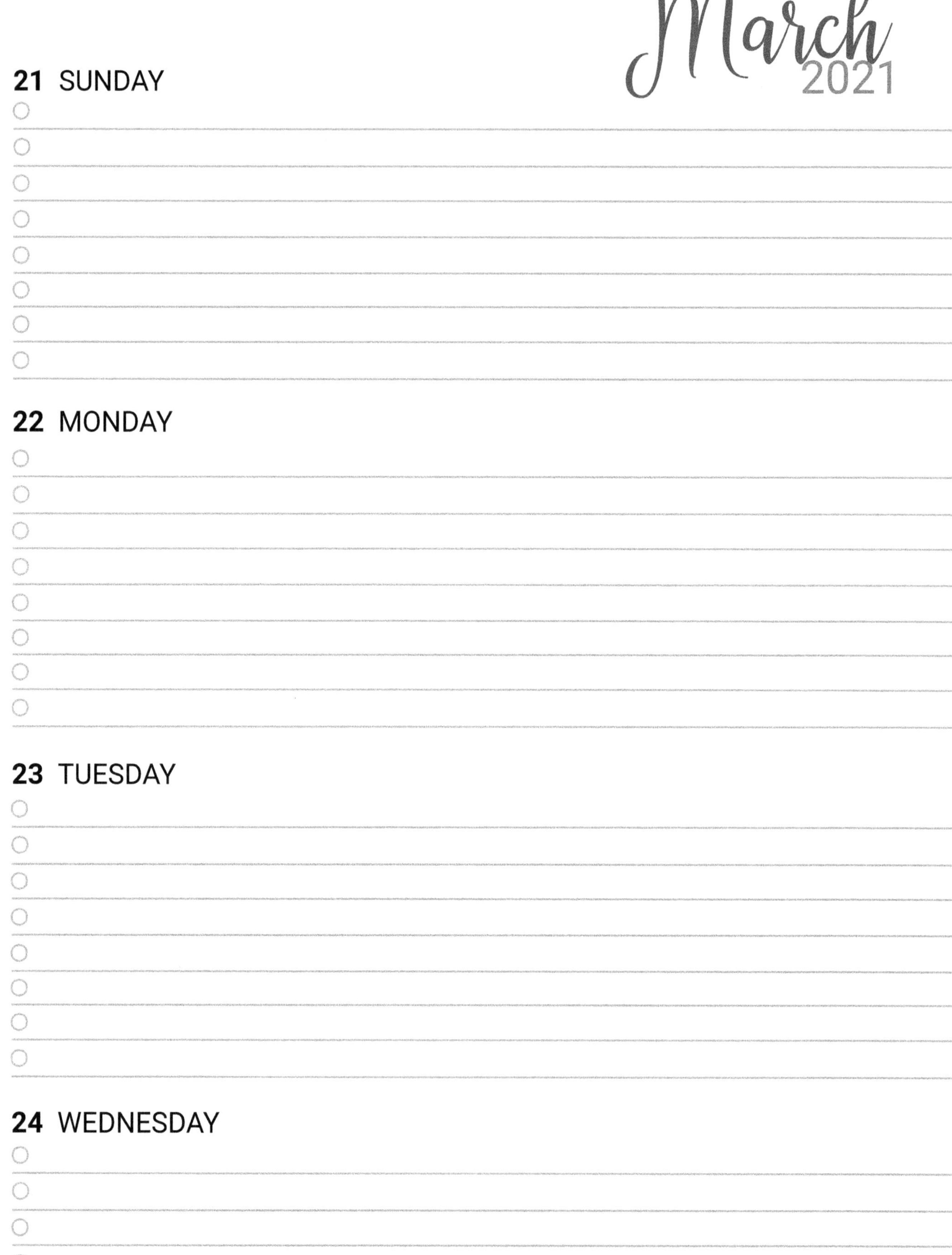



**21** SUNDAY

**22** MONDAY

**23** TUESDAY

**24** WEDNESDAY

**25** THURSDAY

**26** FRIDAY

**27** SATURDAY

**28** SUNDAY

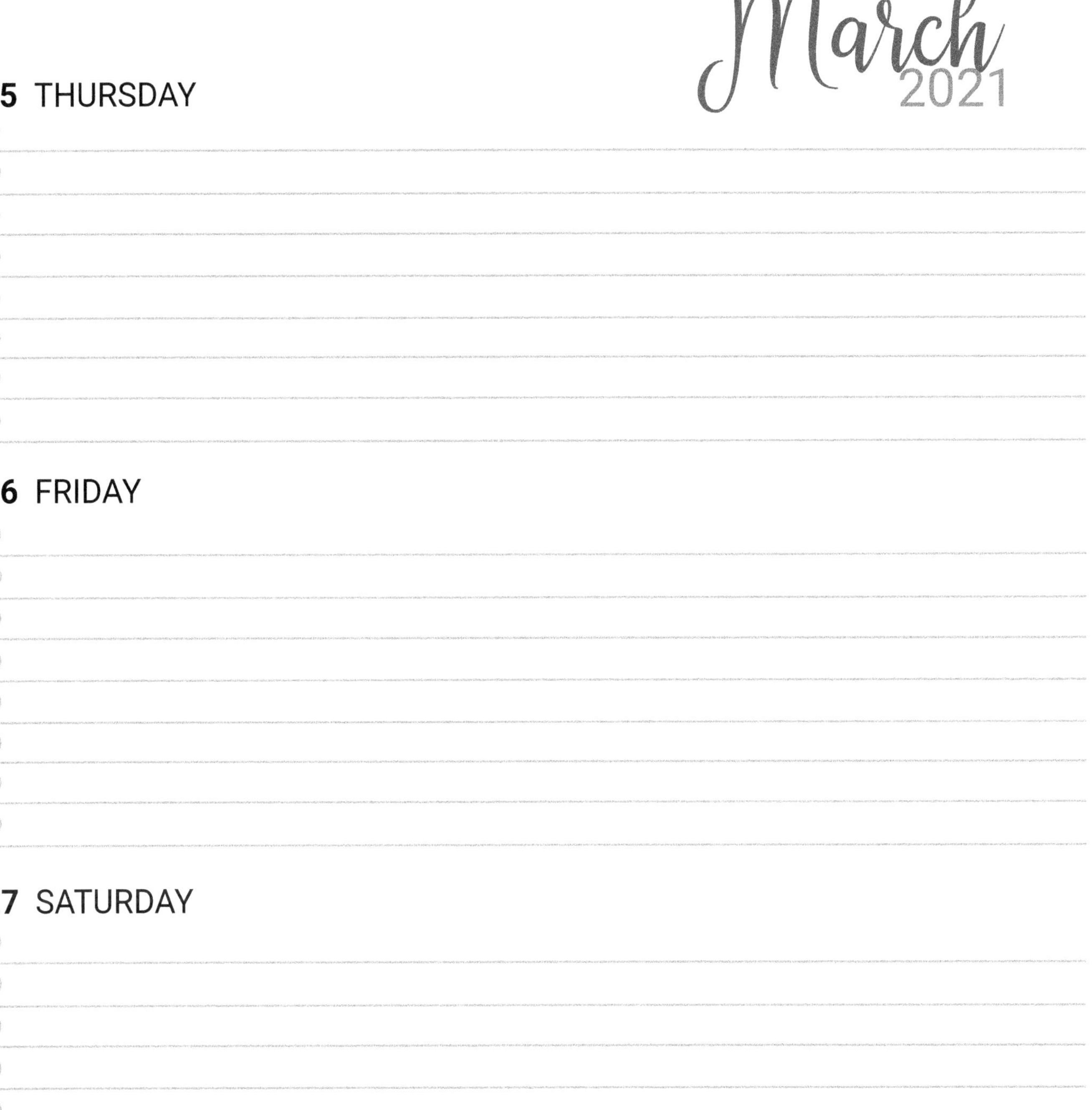

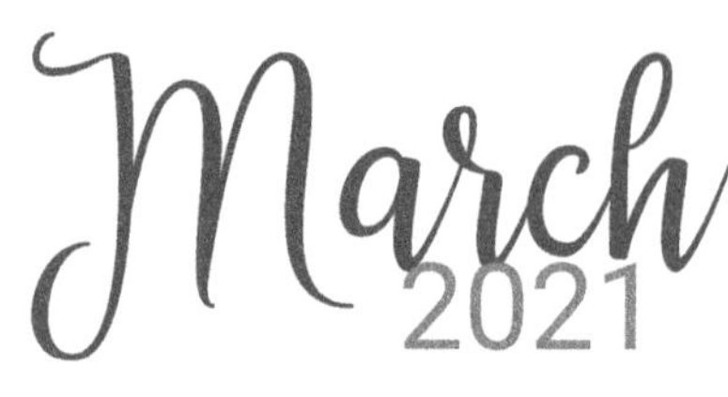


**29** MONDAY

**30** TUESDAY

**31** WEDNESDAY

NOTES

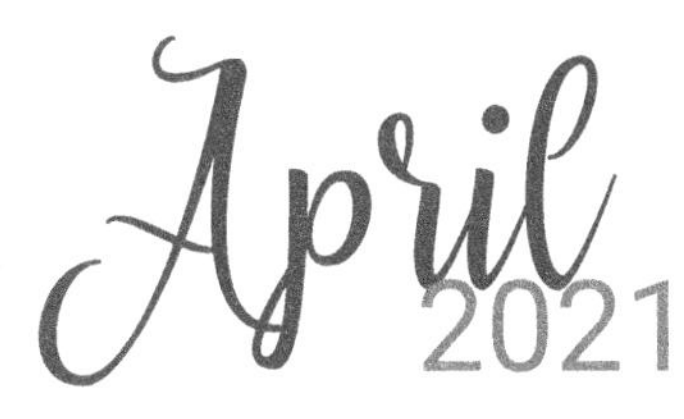

# April 2021

## 01 THURSDAY

## 02 FRIDAY

## 03 SATURDAY

## 04 SUNDAY

**05** MONDAY

**06** TUESDAY

**07** WEDNESDAY

**08** THURSDAY

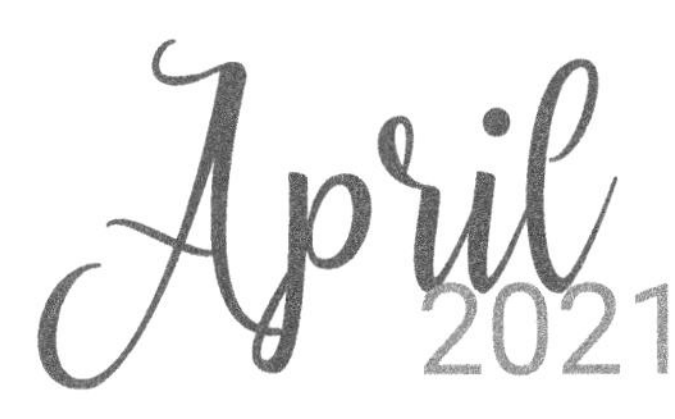


**09** FRIDAY

**10** SATURDAY

**11** SUNDAY

**12** MONDAY

# April 2021

## 13 TUESDAY

## 14 WEDNESDAY

## 15 THURSDAY

## 16 FRIDAY

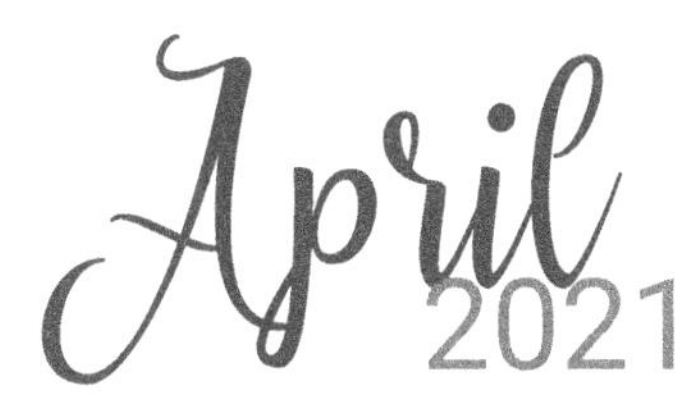


## 17 SATURDAY

## 18 SUNDAY

## 19 MONDAY

## 20 TUESDAY

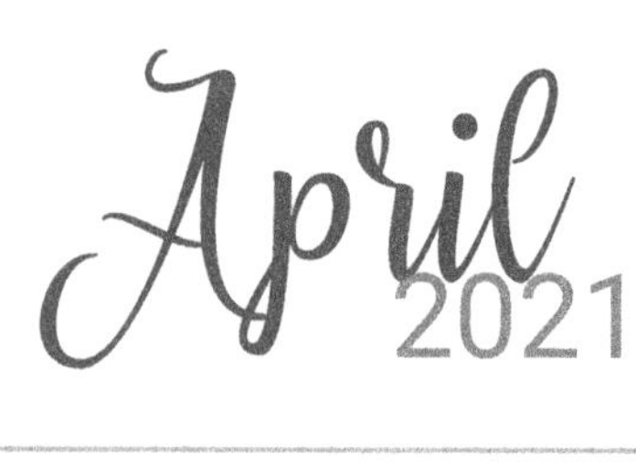


**21** WEDNESDAY

**22** THURSDAY

**23** FRIDAY

**24** SATURDAY

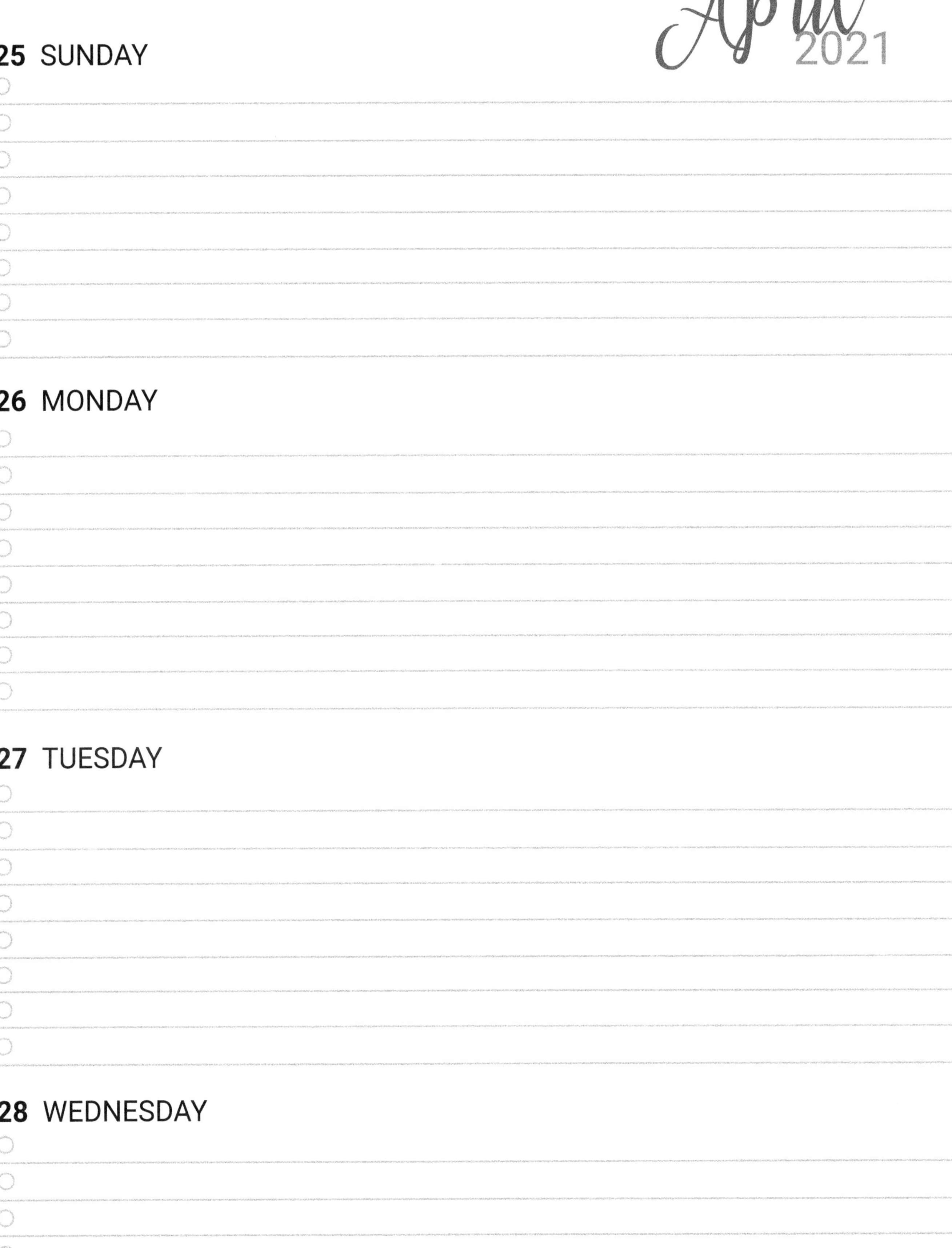



**25** SUNDAY

**26** MONDAY

**27** TUESDAY

**28** WEDNESDAY

## 29 THURSDAY

○
○
○
○
○
○
○
○

## 30 FRIDAY

○
○
○
○
○
○
○
○

## NOTES

# May
### 2021

## 01 SATURDAY

## 02 SUNDAY

## 03 MONDAY

## 04 TUESDAY

## 05 WEDNESDAY

## 06 THURSDAY

## 07 FRIDAY

## 08 SATURDAY

**09** SUNDAY

**10** MONDAY

**11** TUESDAY

**12** WEDNESDAY

## 13 THURSDAY

## 14 FRIDAY

## 15 SATURDAY

## 16 SUNDAY

## 17 MONDAY

## 18 TUESDAY

## 19 WEDNESDAY

## 20 THURSDAY

**21** FRIDAY

**22** SATURDAY

**23** SUNDAY

**24** MONDAY

**25** TUESDAY

**26** WEDNESDAY

**27** THURSDAY

**28** FRIDAY

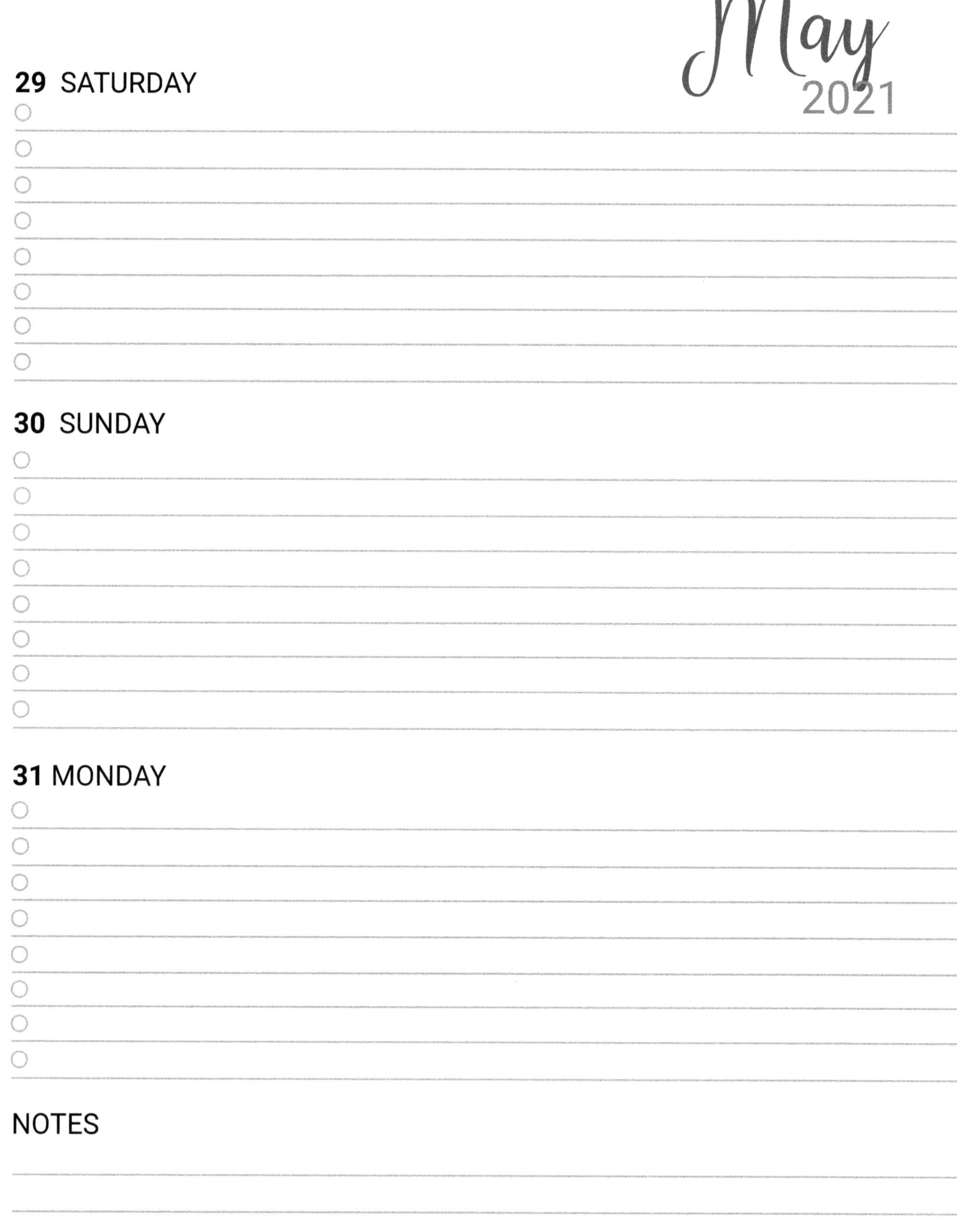

# *May*
## 2021

**29** SATURDAY

**30** SUNDAY

**31** MONDAY

## NOTES

**01** TUESDAY

**02** WEDNESDAY

**03** THURSDAY

**04** FRIDAY

**05** SATURDAY

**06** SUNDAY

**07** MONDAY

**08** TUESDAY

**09** WEDNESDAY

**10** THURSDAY

**11** FRIDAY

**12** SATURDAY

## 13 SUNDAY

## 14 MONDAY

## 15 TUESDAY

## 16 WEDNESDAY

**17** THURSDAY

**18** FRIDAY

**19** SATURDAY

**20** SUNDAY

**21** MONDAY

**22** TUESDAY

**23** WEDNESDAY

**24** THURSDAY

## 25 FRIDAY

## 26 SATURDAY

## 27 SUNDAY

## 28 MONDAY

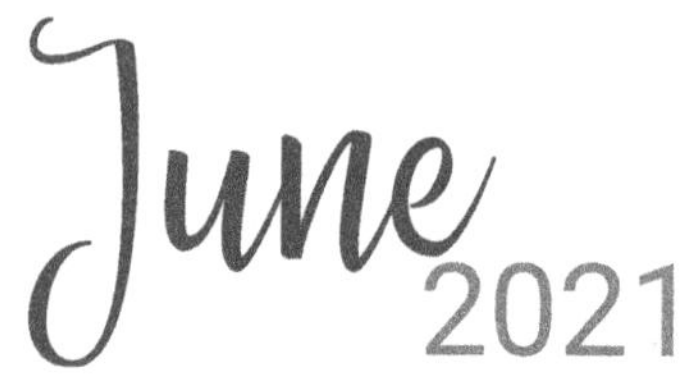

**29** TUESDAY

**30** WEDNESDAY

NOTES

# July

## 2021

**01** THURSDAY

**02** FRIDAY

**03** SATURDAY

**04** SUNDAY

**05** MONDAY

**06** TUESDAY

**07** WEDNESDAY

**08** THURSDAY

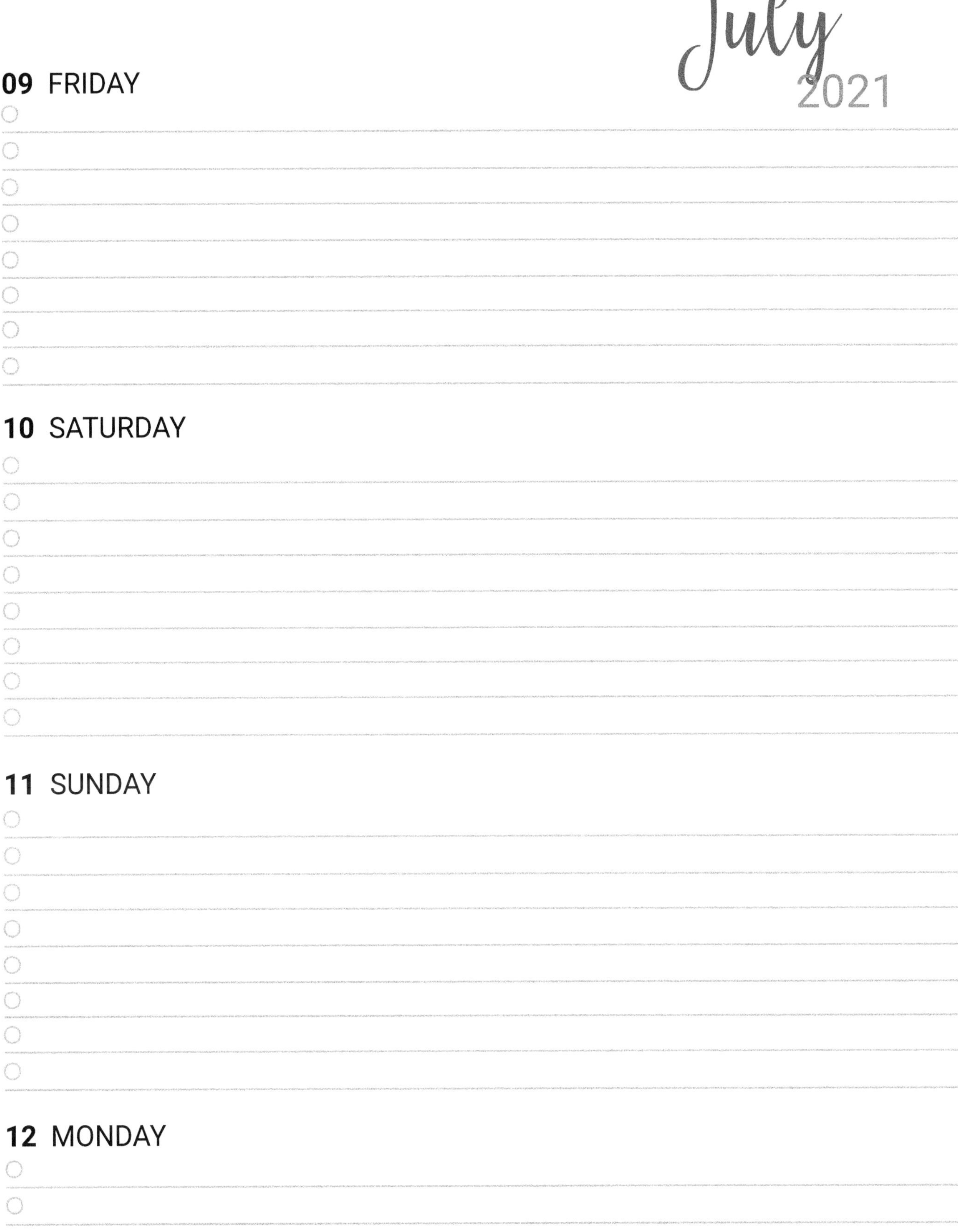

# July 2021

**09** FRIDAY

**10** SATURDAY

**11** SUNDAY

**12** MONDAY

**13** TUESDAY

**14** WEDNESDAY

**15** THURSDAY

**16** FRIDAY

**17** SATURDAY

**18** SUNDAY

**19** MONDAY

**20** TUESDAY

## *July*
### 2021

**21** WEDNESDAY

○
○
○
○
○
○
○
○

**22** THURSDAY

○
○
○
○
○
○
○
○

**23** FRIDAY

○
○
○
○
○
○
○
○

**24** SATURDAY

○
○
○
○
○

**25** SUNDAY

**26** MONDAY

**27** TUESDAY

**28** WEDNESDAY

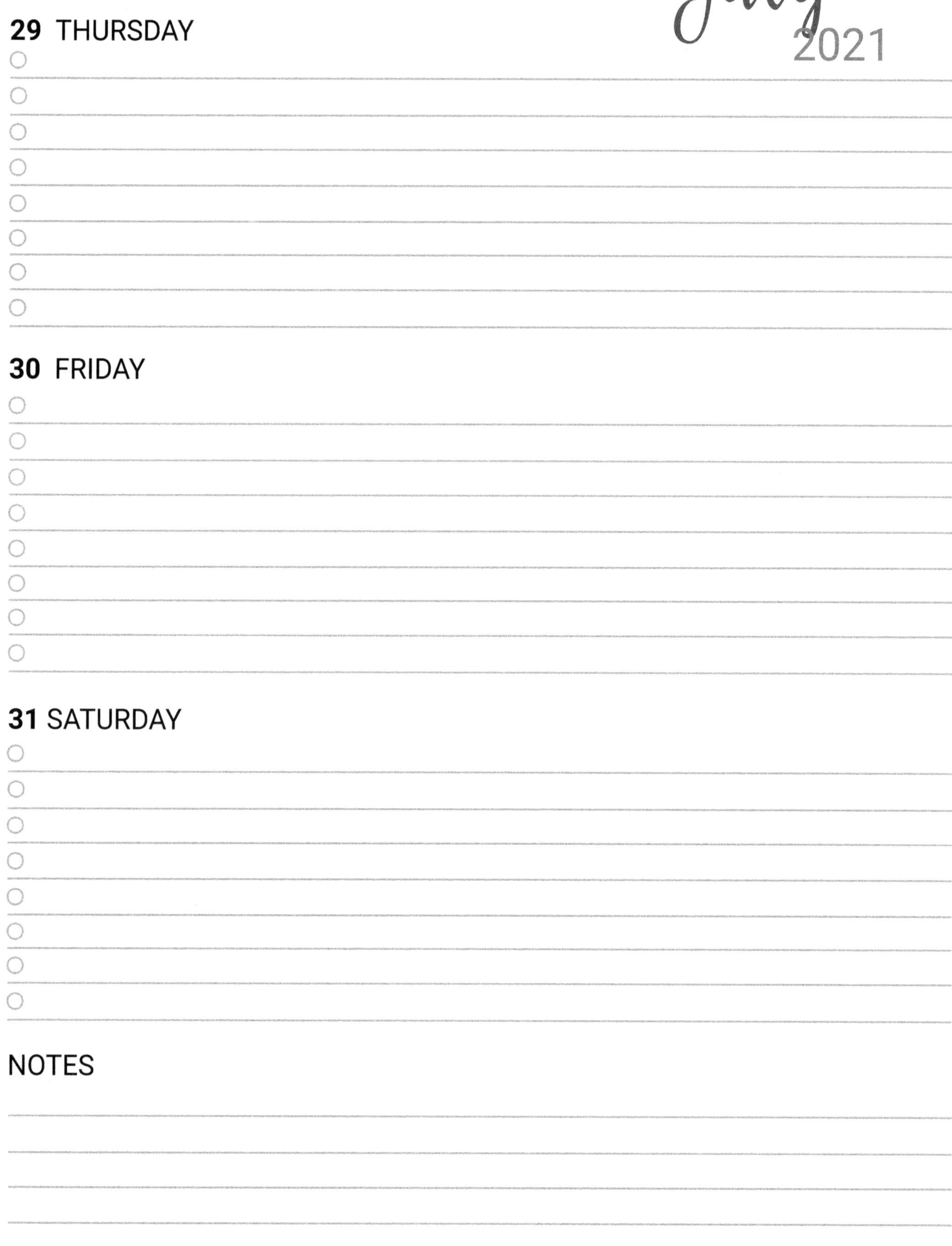



**29** THURSDAY

**30** FRIDAY

**31** SATURDAY

NOTES

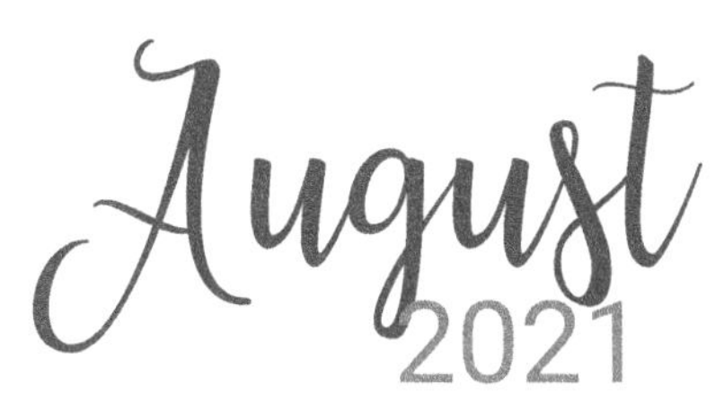



**01**  SUNDAY

**02**  MONDAY

**03**  TUESDAY

**04**  WEDNESDAY

## 05 THURSDAY

## 06 FRIDAY

## 07 SATURDAY

## 08 SUNDAY

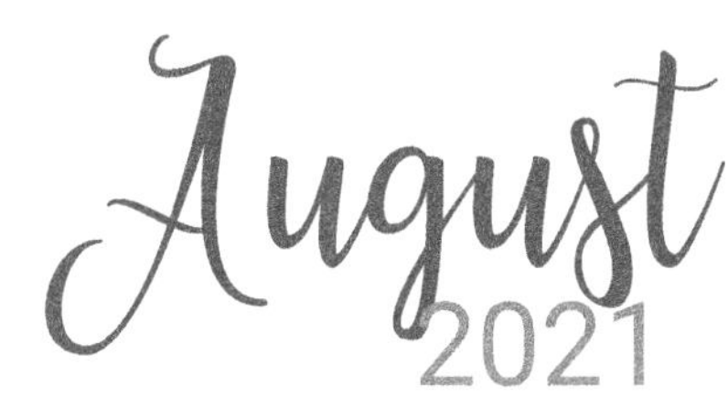

# August 2021

**09** MONDAY

**10** TUESDAY

**11** WEDNESDAY

**12** THURSDAY

**13** FRIDAY

**14** SATURDAY

**15** SUNDAY

**16** MONDAY

**17** TUESDAY

**18** WEDNESDAY

**19** THURSDAY

**20** FRIDAY

## 21 SATURDAY

## 22 SUNDAY

## 23 MONDAY

## 24 TUESDAY

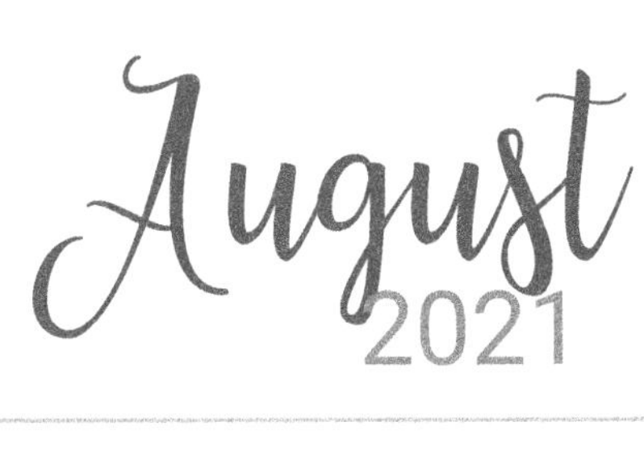

**25** WEDNESDAY

**26** THURSDAY

**27** FRIDAY

**28** SATURDAY

**29** SUNDAY

**30** MONDAY

**31** TUESDAY

## NOTES

**01** WEDNESDAY

**02** THURSDAY

**03** FRIDAY

**04** SATURDAY

# September
## 2021

## 05 SUNDAY

## 06 MONDAY

## 07 TUESDAY

## 08 WEDNESDAY

**09** THURSDAY

**10** FRIDAY

**11** SATURDAY

**12** SUNDAY

# September
## 2021

## 13 MONDAY

## 14 TUESDAY

## 15 WEDNESDAY

## 16 THURSDAY

**17** FRIDAY

**18** SATURDAY

**19** SUNDAY

**20** MONDAY

**21** TUESDAY

**22** WEDNESDAY

**23** THURSDAY

**24** FRIDAY

**25** SATURDAY

**26** SUNDAY

**27** MONDAY

**28** TUESDAY

**29** WEDNESDAY

**30** THURSDAY

NOTES

**01** FRIDAY

**02** SATURDAY

**03** SUNDAY

**04** MONDAY

October
2021

**05** TUESDAY

**06** WEDNESDAY

**07** THURSDAY

**08** FRIDAY

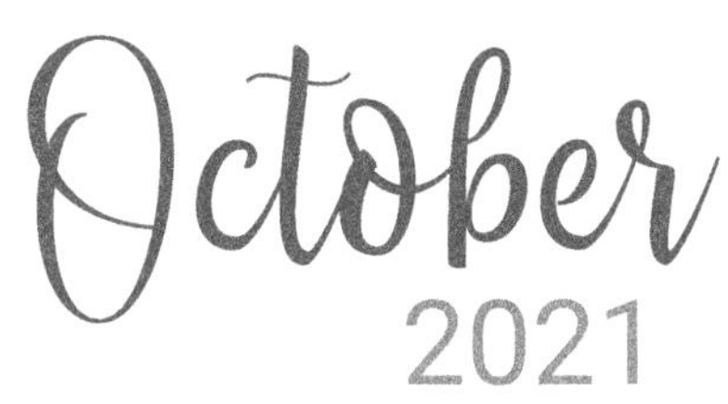

# October
## 2021

**09** SATURDAY

**10** SUNDAY

**11** MONDAY

**12** TUESDAY

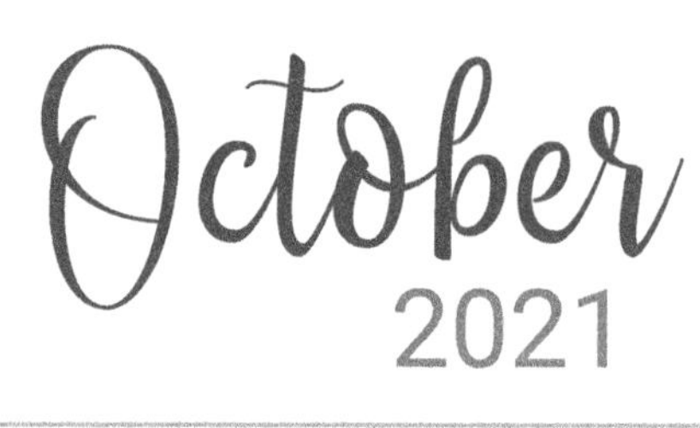

# October
## 2021

## 13 WEDNESDAY

## 14 THURSDAY

## 15 FRIDAY

## 16 SATURDAY

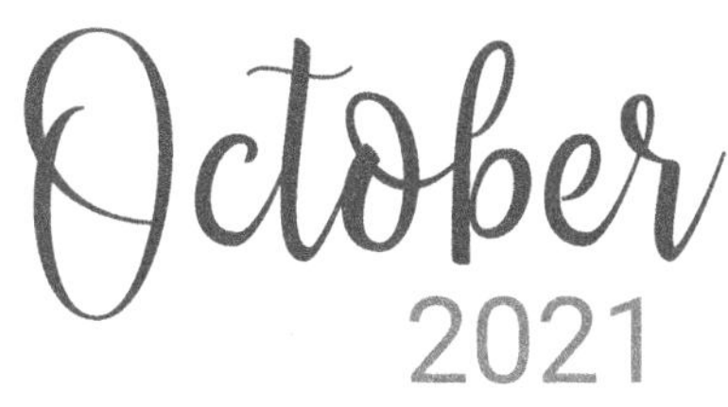

# October
## 2021

**17** SUNDAY

**18** MONDAY

**19** TUESDAY

**20** WEDNESDAY

# *October*
## 2021

**21** THURSDAY

**22** FRIDAY

**23** SATURDAY

**24** SUNDAY

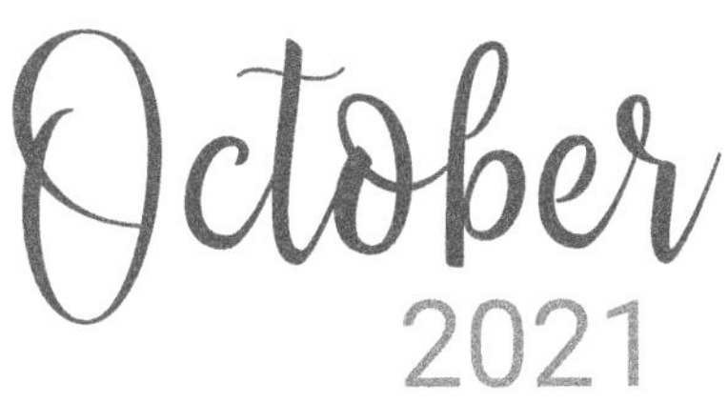

**25** MONDAY

**26** TUESDAY

**27** WEDNESDAY

**28** THURSDAY

**29** FRIDAY

**30** SATURDAY

**31** SUNDAY

NOTES

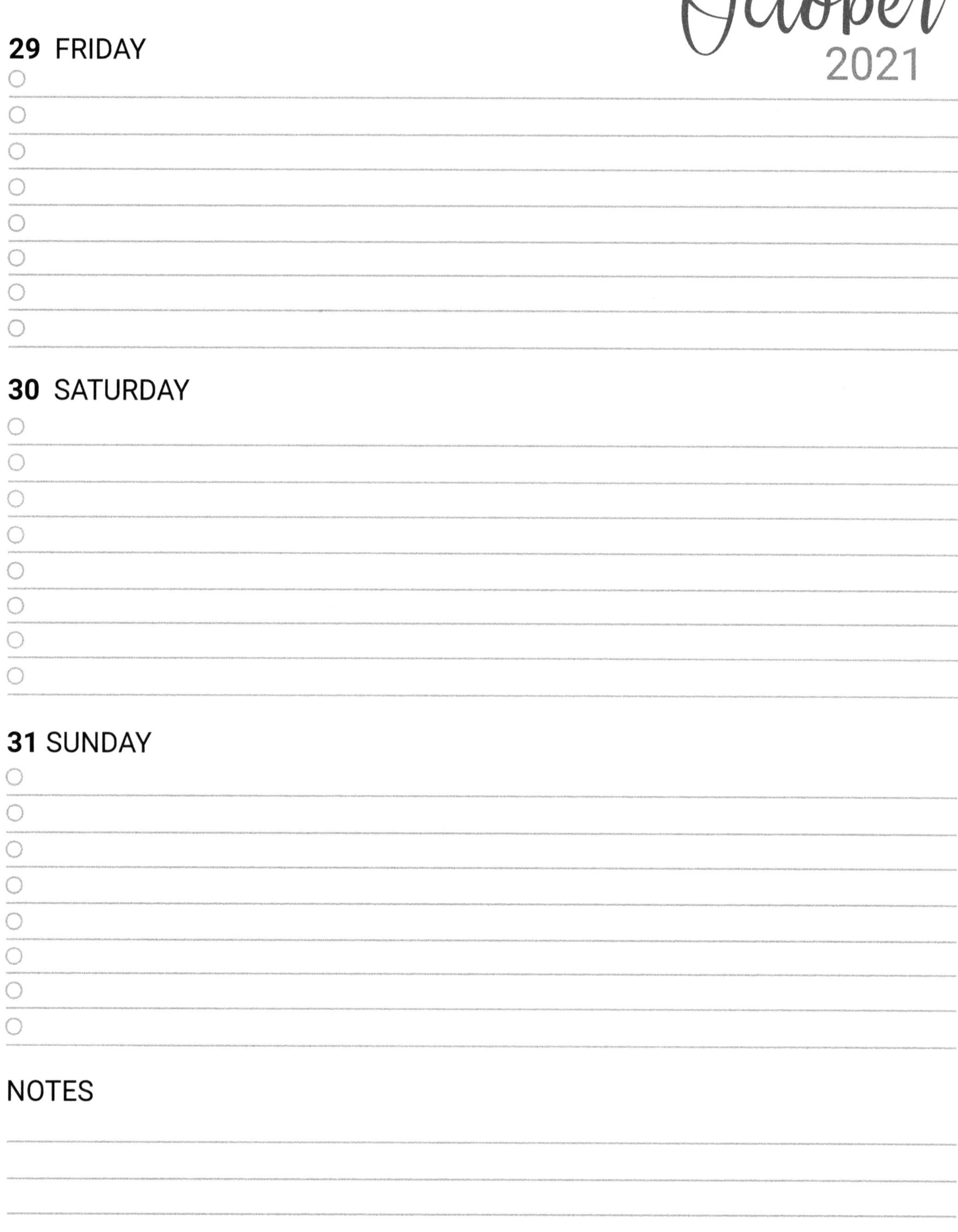

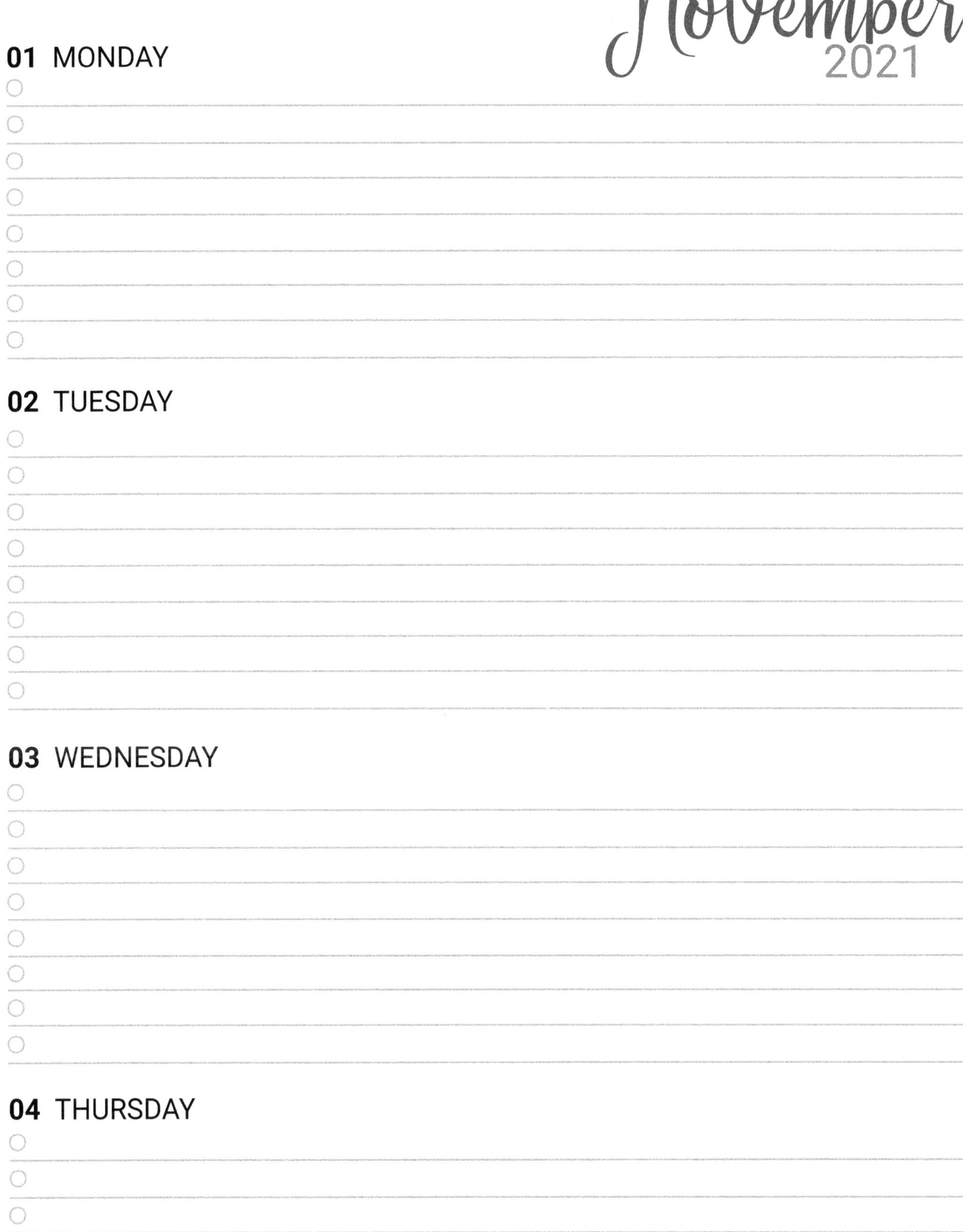


November
2021

01 MONDAY

02 TUESDAY

03 WEDNESDAY

04 THURSDAY

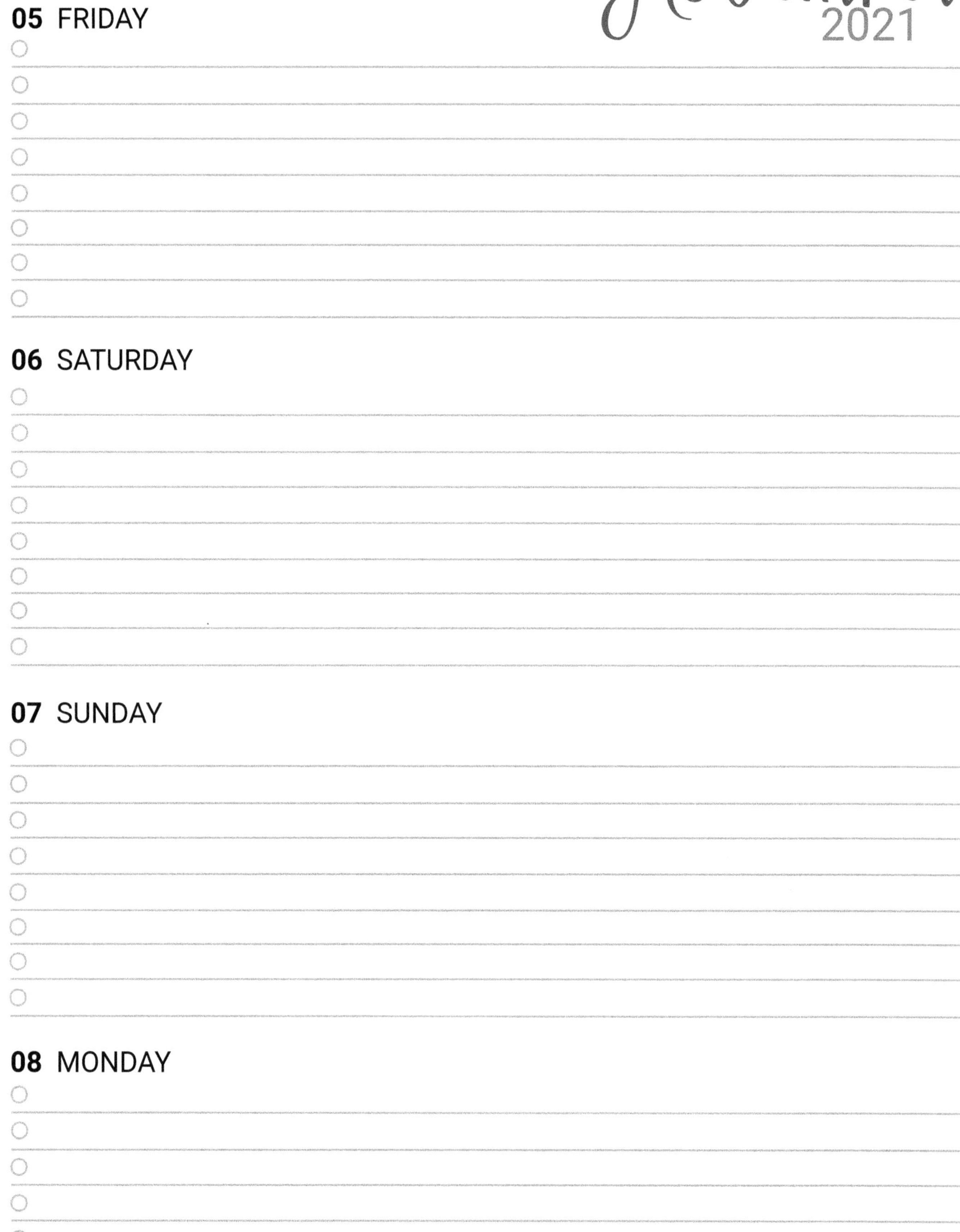



**05** FRIDAY

**06** SATURDAY

**07** SUNDAY

**08** MONDAY

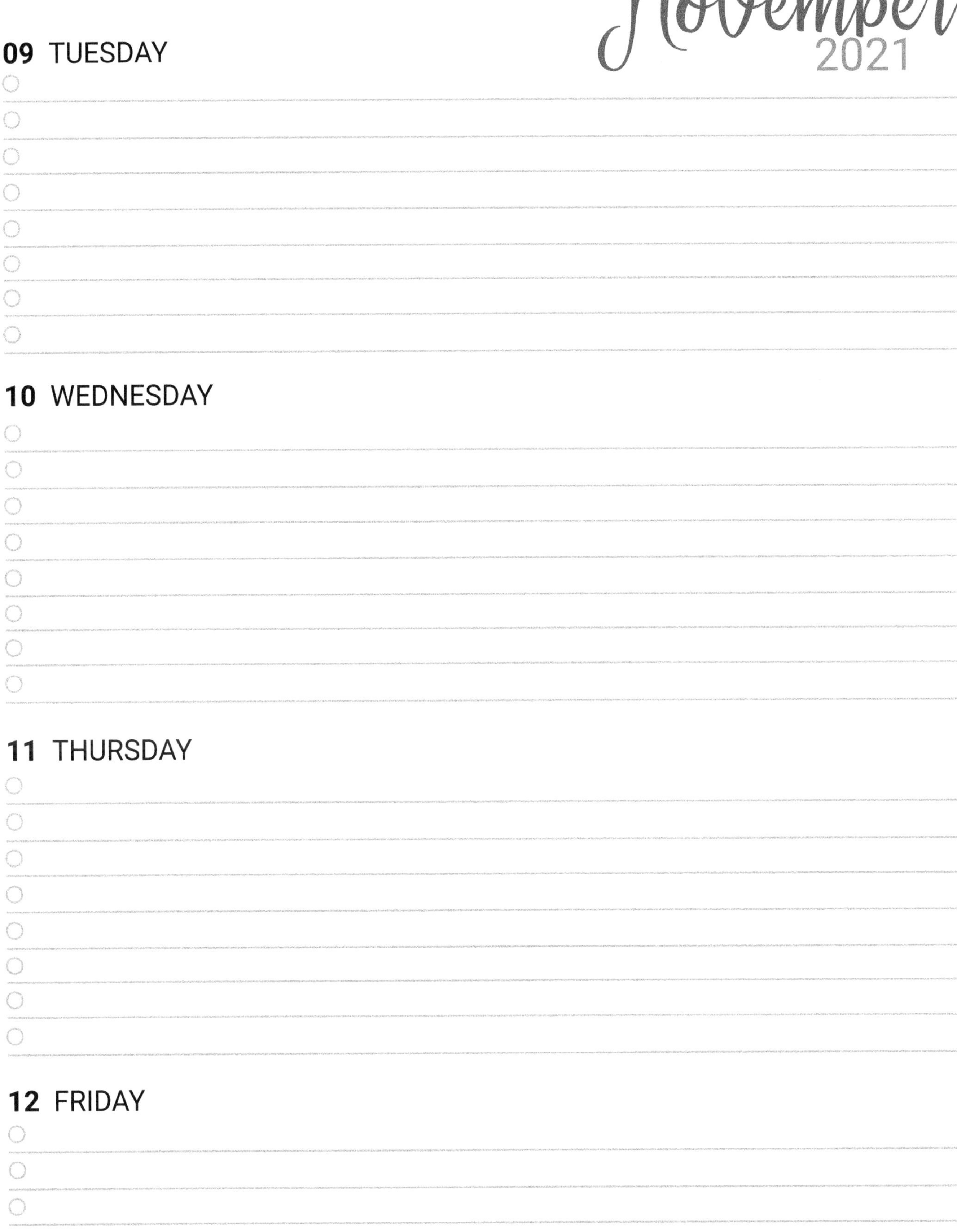

# November
## 2021

**09** TUESDAY

**10** WEDNESDAY

**11** THURSDAY

**12** FRIDAY

## 13 SATURDAY

## 14 SUNDAY

## 15 MONDAY

## 16 TUESDAY

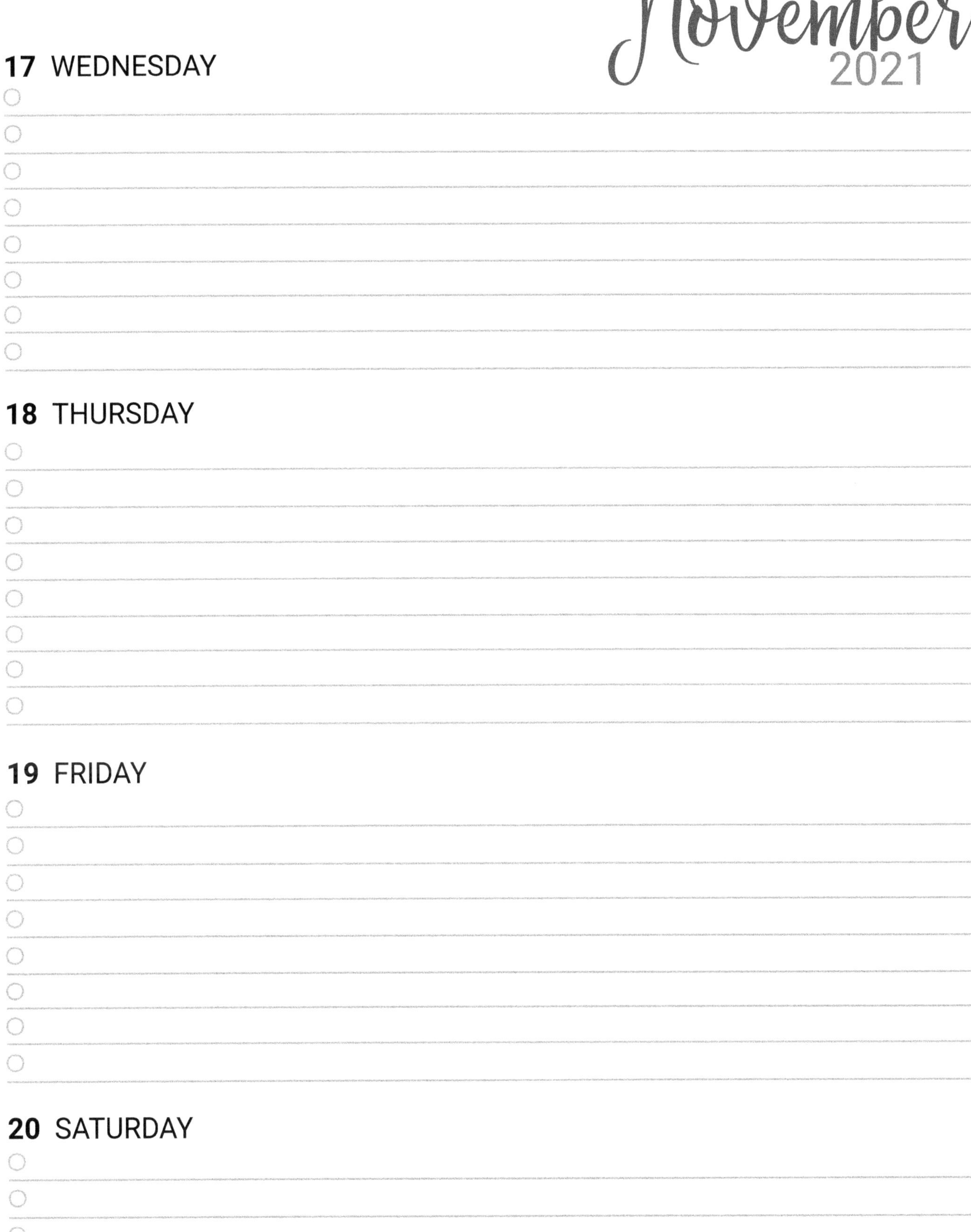

# November
## 2021

**17** WEDNESDAY

**18** THURSDAY

**19** FRIDAY

**20** SATURDAY

**21** SUNDAY

**22** MONDAY

**23** TUESDAY

**24** WEDNESDAY

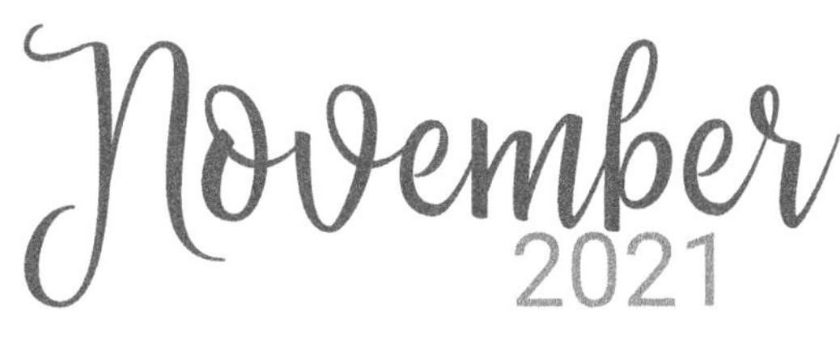


**25** THURSDAY

**26** FRIDAY

**27** SATURDAY

**28** SUNDAY

# November
## 2021

**29** MONDAY

○
○
○
○
○
○
○
○

**30** TUESDAY

○
○
○
○
○
○
○
○

## NOTES

**01** WEDNESDAY

**02** THURSDAY

**03** FRIDAY

**04** SATURDAY

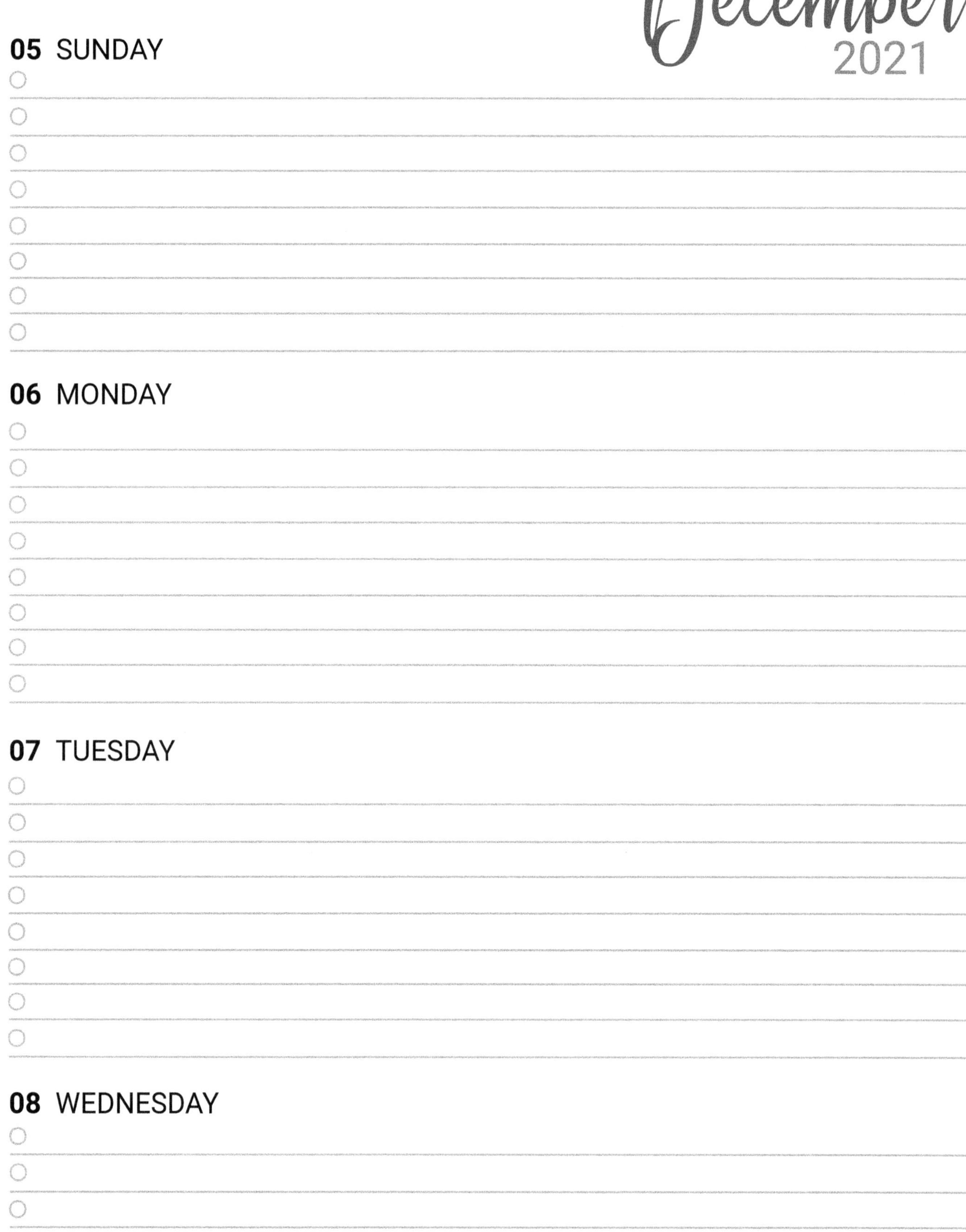

**05** SUNDAY

**06** MONDAY

**07** TUESDAY

**08** WEDNESDAY

**09** THURSDAY

**10** FRIDAY

**11** SATURDAY

**12** SUNDAY

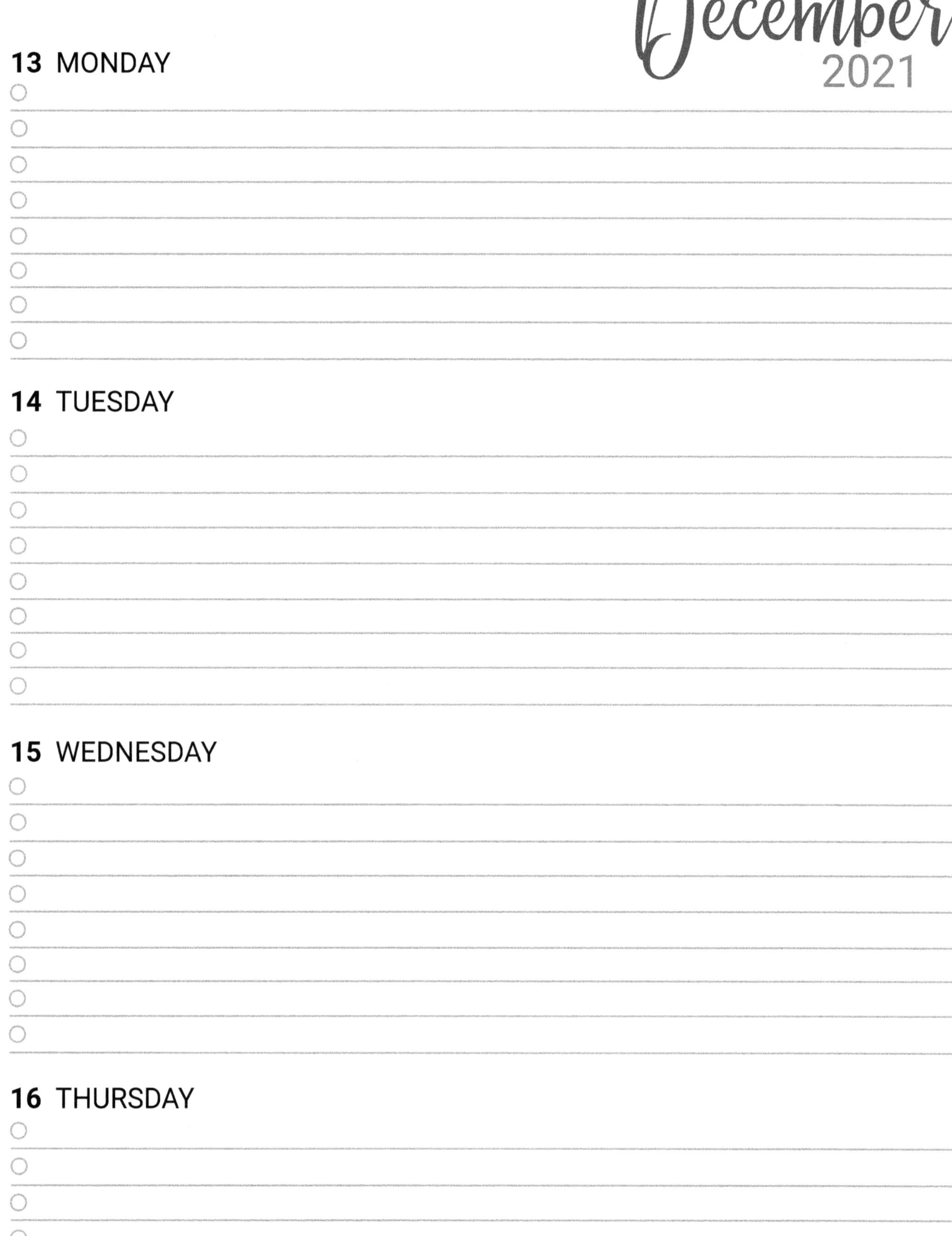

**13** MONDAY

**14** TUESDAY

**15** WEDNESDAY

**16** THURSDAY

## 17 FRIDAY

## 18 SATURDAY

## 19 SUNDAY

## 20 MONDAY

**21** TUESDAY

**22** WEDNESDAY

**23** THURSDAY

**24** FRIDAY

**25** SATURDAY

**26** SUNDAY

**27** MONDAY

**28** TUESDAY

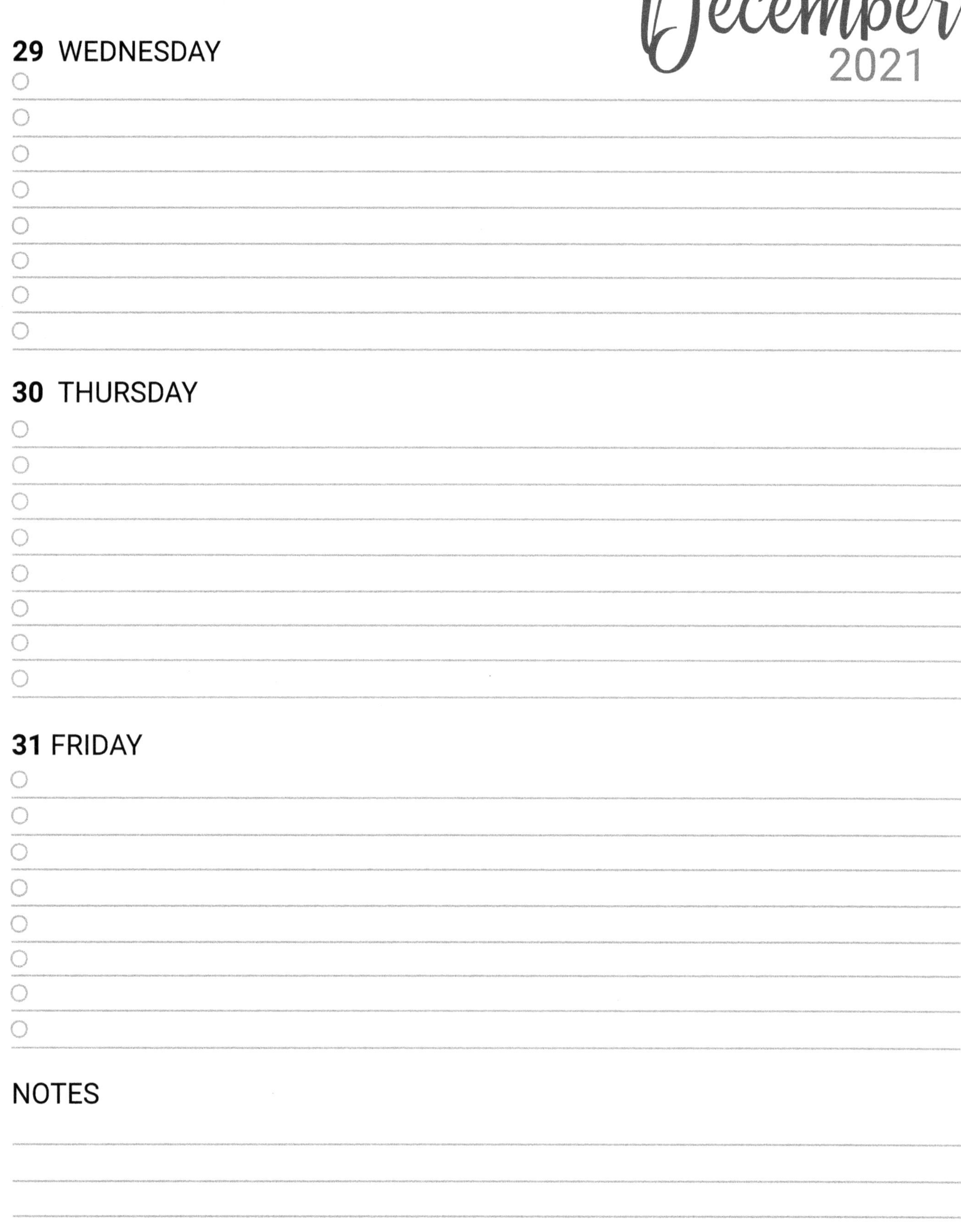



**29** WEDNESDAY

**30** THURSDAY

**31** FRIDAY

NOTES

CPSIA information can be obtained
at www.ICGtesting.com
Printed in the USA
LVHW061528140121
676186LV00018B/672